D1374010

T. S. Chan, DBA
Editor

Consumer Behavior in Asia: Issues and Marketing Practice

Consumer Behavior in Asia: Issues and Marketing Practice has been co-published simultaneously as *Journal of International Consumer Marketing*, Volume 11, Number 1 1999.

Pre-publication
REVIEWS,
COMMENTARIES,
EVALUATIONS . . .

"**C**ustomer attitudes, marketing practices and even ways of looking at problems are culturally conditioned. Professor Chan has produced a text that looks straight at the Chinese market. In doing so, he has provided a replacement for proxy texts that have their roots in research into marketing in other countries."

Kenneth Simmonds, PhD
Professor of Marketing
and International Business
London Business School
England

"**A**s Asian markets beyond Japan become more and more important globally, the need to understand them better increases. Over time we are likely to see the early studies, which were largely limited to providing rough sketches of market and environmental conditions, replaced by more contemporary research that deals with detailed, more focused issues. In this context, this book is likely to become an essential reference for understanding the behavior of consumers in Asia both in and out of itself as well as by comparison to that of their counterparts in North America. Its six chapters deal with a variety of consumer behavior issues with an emphasis on the region's most important market, the People's Republic of China, but also on other markets such as Malaysia, Singapore, and Hong Kong, with three of the chapters providing comparative information using related research in the U.S.A. or Canada.

One of the most impressive aspects of the book is its effective blend of theory and application. The Editor has done a superb job of assembling studies which offer a broad, detailed perspective on consumer behavior. The chapters are very well written, and the statistical methodologies employed in the five studies that report on field research, as well as the conceptual chapter on market segmentation, are solid. The authors approach the central theme from various diverse viewpoints, including buying behavior in the fast-food sector, Asian consumers in the 'Generation X' segment, and cultural issues related to gift-giving behavior. Managers and academic researchers in Western markets will be particularly interested in the two chapters that deal with country-of-origin image issues, in China and in Hong Kong, involving comparative North American research. The views of Asian consumers about the acceptability or desirability of foreign goods will be an important determinant of the future evolution of exports to those two markets. The market segmentation chapter focuses on China but its hybrid approach can serve as a blueprint for understanding and targeting consumer segments in most other Asian countries.

Overall, this book represents a solid treatment of a highly relevant issue in this most important market. Both academics and practitioners will probably find it to be an invaluable reference with considerable staying power as Asian markets continue to evolve and play an ever more important role on the global arena."

Nicholas Papadopoulos, DBA
*Professor of Marketing
and International Businesss
Carleton University
Ottawa, Canada*

"The global marketplace is undergoing vast changes and nowhere are the changes taking place faster than in Asia. Marketers are challenged to keep up with these changes and to assess their implications for developing successful strategies. Arguably, consumption is one of the most powerful influences in today's world. Despite the recent setbacks that Asian markets have experienced, these markets hold enormous potential to effect the course of the world's economic history in the coming millennium. The collection of readings edited by Professor Chan provide many useful insights into elements of consumer behavior of selected submarkets within this region. Marketers and marketing scholars interested in this part of the world will find this eclectic collection of readings worthy of a close look.

There are several readings that are particularly notable within this collection. One of the most compelling articles provides a schema for segmenting the huge Chinese consumer market using a hybird approach of demographics, psychographics, and geographics. . . . Another thought provoking article examines the attitudes of Generation Xers in parts of Southeast Asia toward

International Business Press
An Imprint of The Haworth Press, Inc.

Consumer Behavior in Asia: Issues and Marketing Practice

Consumer Behavior in Asia: Issues and Marketing Practice has been co-published simultaneously as *Journal of International Consumer Marketing*, Volume 11, Number 1 1999.

The *Journal of International Consumer Marketing* Monographic "Separates"

Below is a list of "separates," which in serials librarianship means a special issue simultaneously published as a special journal issue or double-issue *and* as a "separate" hardbound monograph. (This is a format which we also call a "DocuSerial.")

"Separates" are published because specialized libraries or professionals may wish to purchase a specific thematic issue by itself in a format which can be separately cataloged and shelved, as opposed to purchasing the journal on an on-going basis. Faculty members may also more easily consider a "separate" for classroom adoption.

"Separates" are carefully classified separately with the major book jobbers so that the journal tie-in can be noted on new book order slips to avoid duplicate purchasing.

You may wish to visit Haworth's website at . . .

http://www.haworthpressinc.com

. . . to search our online catalog for complete tables of contents of these separates and related publications.

You may also call 1-800-HAWORTH (outside US/Canada: 607-722-5857), or Fax 1-800-895-0582 (outside US/Canada: 607-771-0012), or e-mail at:

getinfo@haworthpressinc.com

Consumer Behavior in Asia: Issues and Marketing Practice, edited by T. S. Chan, DBA (Vol. 11, No. 1, 1999). *Covers several important aspects of these behavior issues, including consumer attitudes and perceptions, market segmentation consideration, marketing communication, and influences of cultural forces.*

Global Perspectives in Cross-Cultural and Cross-National Consumer Research, edited by Lalita A. Manrai, PhD, and Ajay K. Manrai, PhD (Vol. 8, No. 3/4, 1996). *"A thought-provoking collection of chapters by some of the leading academics in the field of international marketing. . . . A useful resource." (What's New in Advertising & Marketing)*

Global Tourist Behavior, edited by Muzaffer Uysal, PhD (Vol. 6, No. 3/4, 1994). *"Could prove very helpful to agents who want to get a better grip on what makes travelers tick." (TRAVEL Counselor Magazine)*

Consumer Behavior in Asia: Issues and Marketing Practice

T. S. Chan, DBA
Editor

Consumer Behavior in Asia: Issues and Marketing Practice has been co-published simultaneously as *Journal of International Consumer Marketing*, Volume 11, Number 1 1999.

International Business Press
An Imprint of
The Haworth Press, Inc.
New York • London • Oxford

Published by

International Business Press®, 10 Alice Street, Binghamton, NY 13904-1580 USA

International Business Press® is an imprint of The Haworth Press, Inc., 10 Alice Street, Binghamton, NY 13904-1580, USA.

Consumer Behavior in Asia: Issues and Marketing Practice has been co-published simultaneously as *Journal of International Consumer Marketing* ™, Volume 11, Number 1 1999.

The development, preparation, and publication of this work has been undertaken with great care. However, the publisher, employees, editors, and agents of The Haworth Press and all imprints of The Haworth Press, Inc., including The Haworth Medical Press® and Pharmaceutical Products Press®, are not responsible for any errors contained herein or for consequences that may ensue from use of materials or information contained in this work. Opinions expressed by the author(s) are not necessarily those of The Haworth Press, Inc.

Cover design by Thomas J. Mayshock Jr.

Library of Congress Cataloging-in-Publication Data

Consumer behavior in Asia : issues and marketing practice / T. S. Chan, editor
    p. cm.
        "Consumer behavior in Asia . . . has been co-published simultaneously as Journal of international consumer marketing, volume 11, number 1, 1999."
    Includes bibliographical references and index.
    ISBN 0-7890-0691-X (alk. paper)
    1. Consumer behavior–Asia. I. Chan, Tsang-sing, 1950-
HF5415.33.A78C66 1999
658.8′342′095–dc21   99-29172
                                                                                                    CIP

INDEXING & ABSTRACTING

Contributions to this publication are selectively indexed or abstracted in print, electronic, online, or CD-ROM version(s) of the reference tools and information services listed below. This list is current as of the copyright date of this publication. See the end of this section for additional notes.

- *Contents of this publication are indexed and abstracted in the ABI/INFORM database*

- *AGRICOLA Database*

- *BUBL Information Service: An Internet-based Information Service for the UK higher education community*

- *Business Education Index, The*

- *Cabell's Directory of Publishing Opportunities in Business & Economics (comprehensive & descriptive bibliographic listing with editorial criteria and publication production data for selected business & economics journals)*

- *CNPIEC Reference Guide: Chinese National Directory of Foreign Periodicals*

- *Contents Pages in Management (University of Manchester Business School), England*

- *Food Science and Technology Abstracts (FSTA) Scanned, abstracted and indexed by the International Food Information Service (IFIS) for inclusion in Food Science and Technology Abstracts (FSTA)*

- *Foods Adlibra*

- *Journal of Health Care Marketing (abstracts section)*

- *Management & Marketing Abstracts*

- *Market Research Abstracts*

- *Marketing Executive Report*

- *Social Planning/Policy & Development Abstracts (SOPODA)*

(continued)

- *Sociological Abstracts (SA)*
- *Textile Technology Digest*

Special Bibliographic Notes related to special journal issues (separates) and indexing/abstracting:

- indexing/abstracting services in this list will also cover material in any "separate" that is co-published simultaneously with Haworth's special thematic journal issue or DocuSerial. Indexing/abstracting usually covers material at the article/chapter level.
- monographic co-editions are intended for either non-subscribers or libraries which intend to purchase a second copy for their circulating collections.
- monographic co-editions are reported to all jobbers/wholesalers/approval plans. The source journal is listed as the "series" to assist the prevention of duplicate purchasing in the same manner utilized for books-in-series.
- to facilitate user/access services all indexing/abstracting services are encouraged to utilize the co-indexing entry note indicated at the bottom of the first page of each article/chapter/contribution.
- this is intended to assist a library user of any reference tool (whether print, electronic, online, or CD-ROM) to locate the monographic version if the library has purchased this version but not a subscription to the source journal.
- individual articles/chapters in any Haworth publication are also available through the Haworth Document Delivery Service (HDDS).

Consumer Behavior in Asia: Issues and Marketing Practice

CONTENTS

ABOUT THE EDITOR

T. S. Chan, DBA, is Dean of Faculty of Business and Chair Professor of Marketing at Lingnan College in Hong Kong. From 1975-1987, he was a Senior Lecturer in Marketing and International Business at the Chinese University of Hong Kong and then relocated to Canada and excelled to Director of Graduate Studies and Research at Saint Mary's University in Halifax. Dr. Chan is active in research and has published six books and over 60 articles and papers in the areas of international marketing strategies, cross-cultural consumer behavior, joint venture decisions, and marketing education. He also serves on the editorial boards of several international journals. His most recent articles have appeared in *Asia Pacific International Journal of Marketing, Columbia Journal of World Business, International Business Review, Journal of Business Communication, Journal of Euromarketing, Journal of Teaching in International Business*, and *Marketing Education Review*.

Introduction

T. S. Chan

As we are evaluating the Asian markets for new developments in the 21st century, we must pay attention to the Asian consumers. This is why this volume focuses on consumer behavior issues in Asia. The six articles included in this collection cover several important aspects such as consumer attitudes and perceptions, market segmentation consideration, marketing communication, and the influences of cultural forces.

The study by Sadrudin A. Ahmed and Alain d'Astous compared Chinese and Canadian male consumers in their judgments of the quality and purchase value of six product categories. Their results showed that both Chinese and Canadians put more emphasis on country-of-design and country-of-assembly information than on brand names when evaluating products. However, unlike the Canadians, the Chinese seem to associate price with quality and put a very high value on return and exchange policy in the case of low involvement products. Both structural and cultural factors were then proposed by the authors to explain the observed cross-national differences.

While country of design and country of assembly are important effects of country-of-origin studies, it is useful to also include the country-of-brand as a factor in influencing product evaluation and consideration decisions. While product consideration is in many cases likely to be related to product evaluation, country-of-brand and brand name information may have somewhat different impacts on each of these constructs. The study by John S. Hulland examined consumer product evaluation, consideration, and rejection in Canada and Hong Kong. Both the country-of-brand and brand name were found to have a significant impact on individuals' overall evaluations. Another important finding that emerged from this study is the incremental impact that some brands have on brand consideration and rejection beyond the effects of country-of-brand. In addition, subjects' evaluations, brand consideration, and rejection all varied systematically by subject nationality.

[Haworth co-indexing entry note]: "Introduction." Chan, T. S. Co-published simultaneously in *Journal of International Consumer Marketing* (International Business Press, an imprint of The Haworth Press, Inc.) Vol. 11, No. 1, 1999, pp. 1-3; and: *Consumer Behavior in Asia: Issues and Marketing Practice* (ed: T. S. Chan) International Business Press, an imprint of The Haworth Press, Inc., 1999, pp. 1-3. Single or multiple copies of this article are available for a fee from The Haworth Document Delivery Service [1-800-342-9678, 9:00 a.m. - 5:00 p.m. (EST). E-mail address: getinfo@haworthpressinc.com].

The study by Michael T. Ewing and Albert Caruana explored the attitudes of Generation Xers in Asia towards advertising. Generation Xers, a moniker coined by post-boom American pop art author Douglas Coupland (1991), represent approximately 21% of the world's population. This new generation of consumers pose a challenging opportunity for global marketers. Although data for this study were collected in Singapore, Malaysia, and Hong Kong, the notion of an Asian Xer is not confined to these more developed countries. Contrary to "Western logic" expressed primarily through North American sentiments towards Xers, this study confirmed an overall positive attitude toward advertising with 85% of respondents considering advertising to be at least somewhat essential. The most important managerial implication for global marketers would be to ignore popular (unverified) stereotypes and look at the Asian markets individually with care.

The emergence of China as a viable consumer market has created tremendous opportunities for international or multinational firms looking for market entry or expansion in China. At the same time, the evolution of the Chinese economy and the increasing heterogeneity of Chinese consumers also pose a great deal of challenges for global marketers trying to assess and evaluate the Chinese market. Geng Cui proposed a hybrid approach in segmenting the Chinese consumer market using demographics, psychographics, and geographics. This approach provided insights in focusing on ways of segmenting China's 1.2 billion population. As China's economy and consumer market continue to evolve, the market place will become increasingly fragmented. The competitive environment will be shifting as well with foreign firms, joint venture operations and local firms competing with new strategies and learning from their successes and failures. The ability to have in-depth understanding of various consumer segments and regional markets in China will greatly enhance the competitiveness of firms looking for long-term prosperity in China.

The study by Patricia M. Anderson and Xiaohong He tested the behavior of Chinese and American consumers with respect to the marketing of fast food. A joint effort of researchers from China and the United States completed two surveys in China and one in the US using a mix of East-, East and West-, and West-influenced instruments. How do consumers compromise on "fast" service versus "food" quality (in terms of taste and nutrition)? What are their preferences? The findings explained the different patterns of purchasing fast food and differentiated the different segments using product preferences and age as segmentation variables. One important implication for doing research in China is that a knowledge of the Chinese culture is needed to understand the extent to which meanings are being attached to words and the implications for consumer behavior.

The last article reported a study by Oliver H. M. Yau, T. S. Chan, and

K. F. Lau on the influence of Chinese cultural factors in gift-giving behavior. With a very elaborate review of the literature in the areas of "face" and "shame," focus group sessions were conducted in Hong Kong to explore the relationships between needs for gift-giving, occasions, consumer choice and decision processes, and Chinese cultural values. A series of propositions were put forth in outlining future research possibilities. This is one of the phases of a major research study which includes various studies across different regions of China to explore regional differences with respect to the impact of cultural forces. With the constructs defined and propositions organized, empirical studies are being conducted to compare Hong Kong (as a Special Administrative Region of China) with other major cities in China to evaluate the implications of Chinese consumer behavior under the One-Country-Two-System Scheme.

Finally, I am indebted to all the reviewers who took time out of their busy schedule to review the manuscripts in a timely fashion. The list of reviewers include: Nick Papadopoious (Carlton University, Canada); Michael Bond, Andrew C. F. Chan, Michael Hui, and H. F. Lau (Chinese University of Hong Kong); David Tse, Oliver Yau, and Nan Zhou (City University of Hong Kong); David Reid (Curtin University of Technology, Australia); Alan Chan (Hong Kong Baptist University); Jamy Joy (Hong Kong University of Science and Technology); Clement Chow (Lingnan College, Hong Kong); Felicitas Evangelista (University of Western Australia); and Ramesh Vanket (Saint Mary's University, Canada). To these friends and colleagues, I express my sincere gratitude.

Product-Country Images in Canada and in the People's Republic of China

Sadrudin A. Ahmed
Alain d'Astous

SUMMARY. This paper presents the results of a cross-national survey of 209 Chinese and 175 Canadian male consumers. In this study, country-of-origin information was manipulated along two dimensions, namely country of design and country of assembly. Consumer judgments of the quality and purchase value of six product categories, i.e., refrigerators, cameras and t-shirts in China, and automobiles, VCRs and shoes in Canada were obtained in a multi-cue context. The results show that Canadian and Chinese consumers put more emphasis on country of design and country of assembly than on brand names in their product evaluations. However, unlike the Canadians, the Chinese seem to associate price with quality and put a very high value on the return and exchange policy in the case of low involvement products. *[Article copies available for a fee from The Haworth Document Delivery Service: 1-800-342-9678. E-mail address: getinfo@haworthpressinc.com]*

Sadrudin A. Ahmed is Professor of Marketing, Faculty of Administration, University of Ottawa, Ottawa, Ontario, Canada K1N 6N5. Alain d'Astous is Professor of Marketing, Faculty of Administration, University of Sherbrooke, Sherbrooke, Québec, Canada J1K 2R1.

The authors would like to thank Professor Yi Hua Wang, Renmin University, for her collaboration to this project and Mr. Li Hu and his wife for their help in preparing the survey materials. The authors' names are presented alphabetically.

Funding for this research study was provided by the Canadian International Development Agency through the Canada-China Management Education Program.

[Haworth co-indexing entry note]: "Product-Country Images in Canada and in the People's Republic of China." Ahmed, Sadrudin A., and Alain d'Astous. Co-published simultaneously in *Journal of International Consumer Marketing* (International Business Press, an imprint of The Haworth Press, Inc.) Vol. 11, No. 1, 1999, pp. 5-22; and: *Consumer Behavior in Asia: Issues and Marketing Practice* (ed: T. S. Chan) International Business Press, an imprint of The Haworth Press, Inc., 1999, pp. 5-22. Single or multiple copies of this article are available for a fee from The Haworth Document Delivery Service [1-800-342-9678, 9:00 a.m. - 5:00 p.m. (EST). E-mail address: getinfo@haworthpressinc.com].

5

KEYWORDS. Product-country images, consumer judgment, Canadian and Chinese consumers

INTRODUCTION

The study of country-of-origin (COO) effects on product evaluations has been a major research stream in international marketing for over twenty-five years (see Papadopoulos and Heslop 1993). In their influential review of this literature, Bilkey and Nes (1982) questioned the validity of previous studies reporting significant effects of COO on product evaluations. The main criticisms made by Bilkey and Nes (1982) were that previous studies had presented COO information in a single-cue format (i.e., only COO information was available), had used verbal descriptions of stimulus products and employed a single dependent variable to assess the impact of the COO cue. These criticisms generated a widespread response and several subsequent studies were designed to overcome these limitations.

More recently, Ozsomer and Cavusgil (1991), Chao (1993) and Samiee (1994) made the observation that the global competitive environment has led to a proliferation of "hybrid" products, i.e., products designed in one country and manufactured in a different country. Such products usually carry brand names with various country connotations and may even be assembled with parts that have been sourced in yet another country. In the present global marketplace context, it is therefore important that researchers interested in studying COO effects distinguish between the country where a product is designed or engineered and the country where it is assembled (Chao 1995). It is also important to adopt a research approach where COO information is presented along with other informational cues such as brand name, price and quality assurance. A few recent COO studies have addressed these research issues but they have been conducted in highly industrialized countries (HICs): e.g., Belgium (Ahmed, d'Astous and Mathieu 1995), Canada (d'Astous, Ahmed and El Adraoui 1993) and the U.S. (Chao 1993). Ahmed, d'Astous and Mathieu (1995) found significant effects of COD and COA on perceptions of the quality and purchase value of three product categories: automobiles, VCRs and shoes. In that study, COD and COA information was presented along with other informational cues (brand name, price and quality assurance) in a conjoint analysis format. The negative perceptions of Mexico and positive perceptions of Canada as CODs and COAs found in a single-cue setting were considerably attenuated when other information on brand name, price and quality assurance was presented along with COO information. Similar results were obtained by d'Astous, Ahmed and El Adraoui (1993) in Canada with the same products using a rating format. Chao (1993) also found significant effects of COD and COA on U.S. consumer evaluations of the design and product quality of a television set.

In order to generalize research findings to the global context, COO studies must be conducted both in HICs, in newly industrializing countries (NICs) and in transitional economies (Ettenson, Kuznetzov and Vetrova 1992; Papadopoulos, Heslop and Beracs 1990; Roth and Romeo 1992). Replication of COO studies in NICs and comparison of results with those obtained in HICs is important. Research has shown that country image perceptions may vary depending on the level of economic development of the country (Papadopoulos, Heslop and Bamossy 1990). In many NICs, especially those with a low per capita income, inefficient marketing systems prevail. Because of low income, individuals are more likely to patronize traditional retail outlets where credit obtainment is easier. Limited storage capacity, the desire of household members to socialize through daily shopping and limited means of transportation all represent factors that hamper the information search process of consumers. For most products, the demand far exceeds the supply and long time established companies tend to be the market leaders. Product information is not freely available and the penetration of mass media and the use of advertisements to promote products are quite limited (Austin 1990). Large differences in market structures and consumer behavior between HICs and NICs are therefore prevalent and COO results obtained in developed countries may not necessarily apply to NICs. This would be particularly true for a transitional economy such as the People's Republic of China (PRC) with its socialistic economic, legal and political systems that grew out of communist doctrine, and with a technological base that is still underdeveloped and resembling that of a NIC (Ralston, Gustafson, Cheung and Terpstra 1993).

The main objectives of this article are: (1) to investigate the effects of three COOs, in the presence of three different brands and three levels of price and quality assurance, on PRC consumers' perceptions of the quality and purchase value of three common product categories, across two dimensions of origin, namely country of design (COD) and country of assembly (COA), (2) to compare the PRC results with those obtained in Canada in order to obtain greater insight into Chinese consumer behavior, (3) to examine the relative impact of brand name versus COO cues cross-nationally, and (4) to discuss the implications of the above for global marketers.

BACKGROUND DISCUSSION

With a population of 1.2 billion, China is the world's largest consumer market. Although China's GDP per capita is $367 (Caetora 1996), the IMF has recently determined that in terms of purchasing power, China's economy is now the third largest in the world after the U.S. and Japan (I.M.F. 1994).

Since the Tiananmen Square incident, there has been an evolution in the values of young Chinese. There is a growing spirit of "Chinese-style" individualism and Western ways of thinking (Ralston, Gustafson, Terpstra, and Holt 1995). Young people dream of a better life, a greater prosperity and the consumption of occidental products (Vear 1996a). This, in spite of constant attempts by the Chinese government to control the contents of radio and television (Vear 1996b) and to prohibit new investments in industries like the tobacco industry (Anonymous 1996). Before the introduction of the economic reforms, the Chinese society was homogeneous with only slight social differentiation. There is now more and more social differentiation based on income, profession or trade (Liping, Hanshang, Sibin and Shanhua 1995).

The PRC transition towards a market economy is rather bumpy. Whereas 3.3 billion U.S. dollars were spent in China in 1995 on advertising (I.M.F. 1996), measures of audiences in T.V. and radio are still lacking, making it difficult to measure the effectiveness of broadcast advertising (Vear 1996b). The quality of Chinese products is felt to be less than desired (Osland and Cavusgil 1996) partly because the expectations of Chinese managers regarding supplier performance are modest (Mummulaneni, Dubas and Chao 1996).

The Chinese and North American cultural systems, i.e., ways of thinking and believing, are very different. Whereas North Americans are rational, scientific, analytical, individualistic and eager for change, Chinese are intuitive, aesthetic, synthetic, and group oriented with a desire for eternity (Xing 1995). Thus, they may be more likely to be influenced by such contextual cues as COO, brand and price in making their purchase decisions. Because of their higher need for cognition, North Americans are less affected by contextual cues (Hague and Bahn 1996). Similarly, the Chinese are more influenced by affect-ladden stimuli than North Americans (Moore, Harris and Chen 1995). Attributes sought from a product and the association of COO or brand name with quality depend on the value system of consumers (Sukhdial, Chakraborty, and Steiger 1995). Evidence suggests that Chinese consumers (Ford, LaTour and Henthorne 1995) and industrial buyers (Kaynak and Kucukemirglu 1992) exhibit purchase behaviors different from those of North Americans.

Canada is a democratic, western country with a long tradition of free market economic principles. Its well enforced legal system enables participants in the market to engage in business and to feel confident that they are protected by a set of well known rules. With a population of 27.4 million, its GDP per capita is 20,774 dollars (Caetora 1996). Comparing Chinese and Canadian data should permit a better understanding of how Chinese consumers' reactions to COO cues differ from those of consumers in an HIC.

Global marketers interested in COO issues in the PRC may obtain some guidance from previous studies available in the marketing literature (see, e.g., Thorelli 1985; Vernon-Wortzel and Wortzel 1987; Yau 1988). However, at the present time there is no study reporting results from the PRC using a multi-dimensional conception of COO in a multi-cue context and making comparisons with a developed country. The present research seeks to fill this gap in the marketing literature.

METHOD

The Canadian data were collected in the city of Sherbrooke, located 90 miles east of Montreal, the second largest city in Canada. Sherbrooke is a mid-sized city (about 80,000 inhabitants) in the French speaking province of Québec in Canada with a strong urban outlook. The Chinese data were collected in the city of Beijing, the capital and principal city of China. Although the choice of these research sites was partly opportunistic (one of the authors who teaches in Sherbrooke was invited to teach at Renmin University in Beijing), both locations represent major urban areas of their respective countries. The data were collected during the Spring of 1993.

Research Design

The product categories selected for the research are refrigerators, cameras and t-shirts in the PRC study and automobiles, VCRs and shoes in the Canadian study. Automobiles and VCRs, cameras and refrigerators are technologically complex and high involvement products while t-shirts and shoes are technologically simple products of daily use in the respective countries. These product categories were chosen in order to allow the generalization of results across products of different levels of involvement, taking into account the level of economic development of a country.

The procedure employed to estimate the impact of COD and COA and the other informational cues is metric conjoint analysis. The conjoint design includes five factors: COD, COA, brand name, price and quality assurance, comprising three levels each. The research design is presented in Table 1. The choice of countries, brand names, product satisfaction assurance and price levels were made in consideration of actual market conditions in Sherbrooke and Beijing. Before going to the field, the research design was pre-tested with convenience samples of Sherbrooke and Beijing male residents. Although some conjoint profiles are somewhat unrealistic, e.g., an $8,000 Toyota automobile designed and assembled in Japan with a 100,000 km/5 years warranty, the respondents (in the pre-test and in the main study) did not experience any difficulty in responding to the stimuli.

Questionnaire

The questionnaire, written in French and Chinese language, consisted of three main parts. In the first part, thirteen countries had to be evaluated as

TABLE 1. Study Design

PRODUCTS

COUNTRIES/ ATTRIBUTES	High Involvement	Medium Involvement	Low Involvement
China	Refrigerator	Camera	T-shirt
Country of Design	China South Korea Canada	China South Korea Japan	China Mexico Canada
Country of Assembly	China South Korea Canada	China South Korea Japan	China Mexico Canada
Brand Name/Store	Xue Hua Mai Er Qin Dao	Ganguang Konika Nikon	Small State Store Large State Store High Quality Store
Price	2,000 yuan 3,000 yuan 4,000 yuan	400 yuan 100 yuan 200 yuan	15 yuan 30 yuan 45 yuan
Warranty/ Satisfaction Assurance	1 year 2 years 3 years	1 year 2 years 3 years	No exchange Exchange only Exchange or refund
Canada	Automobiles	VCRs	Shoes
Country of Design	Japan Canada Mexico	Japan Canada Mexico	Italy Canada Mexico
Country of Assembly	Japan Canada Mexico	Japan Canada Mexico	Italy Canada Mexico
Brand Name (store)	Toyota Ford Hyundai	Sony GE Samsung	Yellow Trans Canada Simard and Voyer
Price	$8,000 10,000 14,000	$300 500 700	$25 35 45
Warranty/ Satisfaction Assurance	1 year/20,000 km 3 years/60,000 km 5 years/100,000 km	1 year 3 years 5 years	No exchange Exchange only Exchange or refund

CODs and COAs using nine-point bipolar scales (poor/excellent). To ensure that the concepts of COA and COD were understood, respondents were provided with descriptive information. COD was defined as the country where the product is conceived, designed or engineered. COA was described as the country where the product is assembled or manufactured. The second part involved the evaluation of nine advertisements of each product defined by combining the levels of the conjoint design factors (see Figure 1 for an example of a Canadian advertisement). The nine ad profiles were defined according to a one-third fractional factorial design confounded with nine blocks (Cochran and Cox 1957). Perceived quality and purchase value were measured with nine-point bipolar scales (very poor quality/very good quality; very bad buy/very good buy). The last part of the questionnaire included questions about product familiarity, product involvement and sociodemographics.

FIGURE 1. Example of an Advertisement Used in the Study

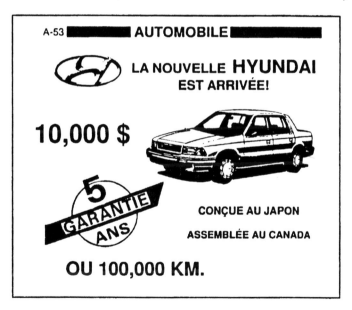

QUELLE EST VOTRE EVALUATION?

TRES MAUVAISE QUALITE   1 2 3 4 5 6 7 8 9   TRES BONNE QUALITE

TRES MAUVAIS ACHAT   1 2 3 4 5 6 7 8 9   TRES BON ACHAT

Data Collection

The data were collected using an area sampling procedure with drop-off delivery. Interviewers visited every second residence of randomly selected streets and asked for residents' participation in the study. In order to be eligible, all respondents had to be males over 18 years of age. This was done because research conducted in less developed countries (Green et al. 1983) and in China (Ford, LaTour and Henthorne 1995) has shown that buying decisions of complex consumer products are often dominated by men. After giving appropriate instructions concerning how to proceed with the materials, the interviewer left the questionnaire with the respondents and picked it up the next day or at a convenient time. In Beijing, from a total of 315 homes visited, there were 34 not at home, 11 with no male over 18, and 45 refusals. Out of the 225 questionnaires left, 219 were collected resulting in 209 usable answers. Chinese respondents were paid a small amount of money for their participation. In Sherbrooke, from a total of 510 homes visited, there were 186 not at home, 34 with no male over 18, and 71 refusals. Out of 219 questionnaires left, 185 were collected resulting in 175 usable answers. No monetary reward was given to the Canadian respondents.

RESULTS AND DISCUSSION

Sample Description

The mean age of the PRC survey participants is 35 years. Twenty-nine percent of them are single, 62 percent have one child, 75 percent have completed high school and 36 percent have some university education. Twenty-nine percent earn under 4800 yuans a year,[1] 60 percent earn between 4800 and 9600 yuans, and 11 percent over 9600 yuans. The mean age of the Canadian participants is 38 years. Thirty-one percent of Canadian participants are single and 56 percent are married. Forty-two percent earn less than 20,000 dollars (Canadian), 40 percent between 20,000 and 49,999, and 18 percent over 50,000. Because of the younger average age of the Canadian sample, the average income is somewhat lower than what one might expect. Thirty-five percent have high school educations and 65 percent have post secondary educations. Thus, the Canadian respondents are wealthier and better educated than the Chinese but the samples are similar in terms of age and marital status.

---

1. At the time the Chinese data were collected, 1 yuan = approximately 0.10 US dollar.

Because better educated people are more likely to participate in complex surveys such as this one, both Canadian and Chinese samples are more educated than the general population. However, a higher than average educated sample is not bad because these often are opinion leaders which make the results more relevant from an applied perspective'.

Manipulation Checks

As expected, the Chinese respondents felt that buying a refrigerator was more important, more difficult and required a greater extent of information search than buying a camera or a t-shirt. The Canadians felt similarly with regard to automobiles versus VCRs and shoes. Buying a camera was perceived as more important, more difficult and requiring more information search than buying a t-shirt by the Chinese and Canadians felt similarly with regard to VCRs and shoes. All differences are statistically significant (p < 0.001).

Country Perceptions

Tables 2 and 3 present the mean ratings of the thirteen countries of origin. Evaluations pertain to perceived design and assembly capabilities of the countries. As one would expect, in general the HICs obtain better evaluations than the NICs. It is interesting to note that South Korea, a newly industrialized country, is rated as highly as Canada as a COD and even higher as a COA by the Chinese. In terms of COA capabilities, South Korea is also rated by the Chinese as highly as Italy and France. With regards to other countries, the Chinese perceptions of the U.S., Russia, and France as CODs are more positive than those of the Canadians but more negative in the case of Canada. As for the evaluation of COA capabilities, the perceptions of Russia by the Chinese are more positive than those of the Canadians but it is the opposite in the case of Canada, Brazil, Mexico and Morocco. In comparison with other NICs excluding Korea, the Chinese rated their own country as superior in terms of both design and assembly capabilities. The Canadians rated the NICs higher on assembly than on design. These differences, in addition to an obvious home country bias, may reflect the greater experience Chinese consumers have with Russian and Korean products and Canadian consumers with products assembled in Brazil, Mexico and Morocco.

The overall low evaluations of NICs observed in the present study are consistent with the findings reported in other country-of-origin studies. According to Li and Monroe (1992), differences in perceived product quality between HICs and NICs are due to consumer beliefs that HICs' workers are more technologically sophisticated than NICs' workers and consequently

TABLE 2. Evaluation of Different Countries of Origin[1,2]

	COUNTRY OF DESIGN			COUNTRY OF ASSEMBLY		
	CHINA	CANADA	DIFFERENCE	CHINA	CANADA	DIFFERENCE
HIGHLY INDUSTRIALIZED COUNTRIES						
JAPAN	7.5	7.4	.1	7.6	7.8	(.2)
GERMANY	6.9	6.8	.1	6.9	6.7	.2
UNITED STATES	7.0	6.7	.3 *	7.0	6.8	.2
CANADA	5.6	6.8	(1.2) **	5.7	7.0	(1.3) **
FRANCE	6.5	5.9	.6 **	6.1	6.1	—
ITALY	6.2	6.1	.1	6.1	5.9	.2
MEAN	6.6	6.6	—	6.5	6.7	(.2)
NEWLY INDUSTRIALIZED COUNTRIES						
SOUTH KOREA	5.7	4.6	1.1 **	6.1	5.2	.9 **
CHINA	4.4	NIL	NIL	4.6	NIL	NIL
BRAZIL	4.1	4.1	—	4.3	4.6	(.3) *
MEXICO	4.2	4.1	.1	4.3	4.9	(.6) **
MOROCCO	4.0	3.9	.1	4.1	4.4	(.3) *
INDIA	3.6	3.6	—	3.9	4.0	(.1)
RUSSIA	3.9	3.3	.6 **	4.5	3.9	.6 **
MEAN	4.0	3.8	.2	4.3	4.4	(.1)

[1]Scale values range from 1 to 9.
[2]Raw scores for PRC respondents adjusted for positive response bias.
*Statistically significant at $p \leq 0.05$.
**Statistically significant at $p \leq 0.01$.

more capable of making quality products. Apparently, PRC consumers share the views held by American and European consumers.

These preliminary results indicate that Chinese consumers evaluate Korea and Russia more positively as COOs than Canadian consumers. A similar finding was reported by Kaynak and Kucukemirglu (1992) with industrial buyers. This favourable evaluation by Chinese respondents may be due to their greater experience with the products made in these countries. The relatively poor evaluation of Canada as a COO by the Chinese may perhaps be attributed to their limited experience with Canada, its people and its products. Research findings indicate that consumers use the COO cue symbolically by associating countries with their areas of excellence: Denmark with agriculture, France with fashion and design, Germany with technology and engi-

TABLE 3. Evaluation of Different Countries of Origin (Assembly Minus Design)

	ASSEMBLY minus DESIGN					
	CHINESE		CANADIANS		INTER-GROUP DIFFERENCES	
DEVELOPED COUNTRIES						
JAPAN	.1		.3	*	(.2)	
GERMANY	—		(.1)		.2	
U.S.A.	—		.1		(.1)	
CANADA	—		.2		(.1)	
FRANCE	(.4)	*	.1		(.5)	**
ITALY	(.1)		(.1)		—	
MEAN	(.1)		.1		(.27)	
NEWLY INDUSTRIALIZED COUNTRIES						
SOUTH KOREA	.3	*	.6	**	(.3)	
CHINA	.3	*	NIL		NIL	
BRAZIL	.2		.4	**	(.2)	
MEXICO	.1		.8	**	(.7)	**
MOROCCO	.1		.5	**	(.4)	**
INDIA	.2	*	.4	**	(.2)	
RUSSIA	.5	**	.5	**	—	
MEAN	.2	*	.5	**	(.3)	

*Statistically significant at $p \leq 0.05$.
**Statistically significant at $p \leq 0.01$.

neering, and so on (Niss 1996). Presumably, no such symbolic association has yet been formed in China with regards to products designed and/or assembled in Canada.

Evaluations of Product Profiles

Table 4 presents the ANOVA results associated with the evaluations of product profiles. Only the main effects are presented since the interactions were not statistically significant. The results indicate that the effects of COD and COA on the perceived quality of all products are statistically significant. As for the purchase value dependent variable, the effects of COA and COD are significant except for the impact of COD on the purchase value perceptions of t-shirts in the Chinese sample. Brand name explains a small but

TABLE 4. ANOVA Results: Mean Squares and Statistical Significance Levels

a) Perceived Quality Source of Variation	CHINA	CANADA	CHINA	CANADA	CHINA	CANADA
	Refrigerator	Automobile	Camera	VCRs	T-shirt	Shoes
Country of Design	21**	162**	278**	257**	30**	159**
Country of Assembly	18**	95**	177**	125**	48**	102**
Brand Name	25**	114**	23**	27**	—	30**
Price	7	8	35**	5	72**	2
Quality Assurance	1	40**	2	15**	92**	1

b) Purchase Value Source of Variation						
Country of Design	24**	107**	276**	175**	8	143**
Country of Assembly	22**	144**	210**	139**	48**	94**
Brand Name	25**	86**	36**	31**	1	29**
Price	21**	39**	5	72**	1	24**
Quality Assurance	26**	129**	11*	89**	427**	24**

*Statistically significant at $p < 0.05$.
**Statistically significant at $p < 0.01$.

statistically significant portion of the variance in the perceptions of quality and purchase value of VCRs, shoes, cameras and refrigerators, has no impact on the evaluations of t-shirts, and plays an important role in the evaluation of automobiles. Satisfaction assurance (warranty) has a statistically significant impact on purchase value perceptions of all six products. The impact of satisfaction assurance on t-shirt evaluations by the Chinese is substantial, especially in the case of the purchase value dependent variable. Satisfaction assurance is a more important factor in the evaluation of high involvement products by Canadians: its impact on the perceived quality of VCRs and automobiles (products evaluated by the Canadians) is statistically significant whereas it is not in the case of cameras and refrigerators (products evaluated by the Chinese). Although satisfaction assurance has a significant impact on the purchase value perceptions of all products, the mean squares associated with VCRs and automobiles have a much greater magnitude than those associated with cameras and refrigerators. Satisfaction assurance is the most important cue in Chinese perceptions of the quality and purchase value of t-shirts. In the Chinese sample, price has a statistically significant impact on the perceived quality of cameras and t-shirts and on the purchase value of refrigerators. For Canadians, price is significantly related to purchase value perceptions of VCRs, automobiles and shoes but not with their perceived quality. Thus, one may speculate that price tends to be an indicator of value for the Canadians, whereas it may be an indicator of product quality for the

Chinese. Using the magnitude of mean squares as an indicator of effect strength, it can be seen that COD and COA are much more important cues than brand name for both Canadian and Chinese consumers. In the case of t-shirts, a product evaluated by the Chinese, satisfaction assurance is the most important cue, especially in judgments of purchase value. Thus, on an overall basis, there appear to be considerable differences between the Chinese and the Canadians in the way price and satisfaction assurance cues impact on product perceptions.

These cross-national differences are believed to be partly due to China still undergoing the transformation from a centrally planned to a market economy. Although marketing technology is being transferred to the PRC, the process is just starting. Brand/store names are just beginning to establish their franchise. Known foreign brand names are probably better indicators of their countries of origin than of the reputation of the products' manufacturer (Harris, Garner-Earl, Sprick and Carroll 1994). In the absence of reliable brand information (Maheswaran 1994) and given the expected variance in the durability of t-shirts in China, satisfaction assurance becomes an important extrinsic cue for judging quality and especially purchase value. It is also interesting to note that for two product classes, namely cameras and t-shirts, where foreign brand names were present, price was an indicator of quality in China. Thus, it appears that PRC consumers do search for reliable extrinsic cues to make their purchase task less complex but seem less likely to use satisfaction assurance to evaluate the quality of high involvement products as do the Canadians.

Overall, it would appear that the differences between Chinese and Canadian consumers' use of extrinsic contextual cues are driven both by structural factors and by cultural differences. Chinese people are group oriented (Xing 1995). Therefore, possession of a high-priced product represents a means of satisfying a deep seated social value. In contrast with this culturally driven cross-national difference between Canadians and Chinese in the importance given to price, the greater importance given to satisfaction assurance for such low involvement products as t-shirts by the Chinese can be attributed to structural factors. The quality of products made in China is less than desired (Osland and Cavusgil 1996). At the same time, the expectations of Chinese managers regarding supplier performance are modest (Mummulaneni, Dubas and Chao 1996). Therefore, because of the greater likelihood of encountering poor quality products in stores, it is quite understandable that Chinese consumers place a high value on being able to exchange and even get a refund for a bad product purchase. On the other hand, in Western countries the expectations of purchase managers are far more stringent with regards to supplier performance (Mummulaneni, Dubas and Chao 1996), so they would be expected to exercise much greater control on the quality of products. So the value of exchange and refund for low involvement products (such as shoes) is low in a country like Canada because consumers probably expect few problems with the products purchased. Yet another reason why exchange/refund for t-shirts plays a greater part in the evaluations of Chinese consumers is because this type of product satisfaction assurance for low involvement products is not prevalent.

The higher need for cognition by Canadians may explain why satisfaction assurance has a significant impact on perceived product quality for medium and high involvement products. Using a rational and analytic way of thinking, why would a company engage itself in providing a long-term warranty unless its products were really durable? The costs of product repair is high in Canada and thus warranty implies a better quality control on the part of manufacturers. On the other hand, because of their limited experience with marketing tactics, the Chinese may have felt that product warranty was just a promotional device for selling products. It is also possible that, because the cost of labour is so low in China in comparison with Canada, Chinese consumers do not believe that offering a long-term warranty necessarily implies that manufacturers provide better quality products.

MANAGERIAL AND RESEARCH IMPLICATIONS

This research suffers from a number of limitations. It was carried out in only one PRC and one Canadian city using different sets of products with an all-male consumer sample. Our results must therefore be interpreted with great care. Further research should be conducted with larger probabilistic samples from different parts of the PRC and HICs and use other categories of products. These studies would be useful to global marketers interested in the PRC who want information concerning issues such as whether or not it makes sense to export products designed in a HIC and assembled in a NIC to the PRC, or to manufacture HIC-designed products in the PRC. Because China is a very large country, future researchers may not only wish to replicate this type of study in various regions of China but also measure relevant cultural differences between China and HICs directly rather than imputing them as was done in the present study. Despite these limitations, we believe that the results presented in this paper have strategic implications for global marketers.

Our results show that brand name is a less important cue than COD and COA in explaining product perceptions in Canada and in China. Satisfaction assurance is a very strong marketing tool for products like t-shirts whose manufacture in the PRC is dominated by public sector enterprises and counterfeit foreign brands (Harvey and Ronkainen 1985). Global marketers who manage to build a strong brand franchise for their products now and stop counterfeiters from using their brand name should be able to reap benefits in the future. Advertising, satisfaction assurance, counterfeit surveillance and other marketing tools used to sell brands should be viewed as an investment made to create brand franchise rather than as marketing expenditures. This long term marketing investment may lead to large benefits as the transitional nature of the PRC economy ends and the PRC takes on the trappings of a fully fledged market economy.

It is interesting to note that, in some instances, price is an indicator of quality for the Chinese. Therefore, selling a HIC product at a low price may perhaps create dissonance for Chinese consumers. Selling a high quality (new) product at low price to capture a large share of the Chinese market may not necessarily be a good strategy. In contrast, price is seen as a value feature in Canada. This perhaps explains why many global corporations that assemble their products in NICs are able to sell their products on the Canadian market by offering competitive prices. Global marketers who have both NIC and HIC manufacturing operations are advised to show caution in exporting their NIC assembled products to the PRC. The Chinese not only put low importance on price as a cue for judging the purchase value of products but they also have a much lower evaluation of NICs such as Mexico, Brazil and Morocco as COAs.

Because of the transitional nature of the Chinese economy, many COOs such as Canada that have highly sophisticated design and assembly operations are not known to Chinese consumers. Therefore in selling their products, these countries should make consumers aware of the quality of their design and assembly capabilities. This can be done through the mass media, advertising campaigns, some very active participation in trade fairs and the provision of free product samples to Chinese opinion leaders. Given the size of the Chinese market and the rapid growth of the income of Chinese consumers, countries that manage to successfully close the gap between the actual quality of their products and the relatively less favorable impression that Chinese consumers have of these products, will reap very important benefits over time.

More specifically, in the case of the North American Free Trade Agreement, U.S. branded products are increasingly being manufactured in both Canada and Mexico. Our results suggest that it may perhaps be advisable for multinational companies to export U.S. designed products to China that are also assembled in the U.S. until the brand equity of the new product is established and COA becomes less important to Chinese consumers. Given that China is evaluated more favourably by the Chinese as a COA than Mexico, U.S. and Canadian corporations may perhaps find it advantageous to assemble their products in China for the Chinese market rather than export products assembled in Mexico. Chinese consumers perhaps because of their greater positive experience with neighbouring countries appear to show a stronger preference for products made in their own country. For example, South Korea is perceived to be at least as good as Canada, France or Italy as a COA. Therefore, a global organization that already has assembly operations in the region surrounding China may be well advised to export its products to China from these locations rather than from medium prestige HICs or non-regional NICs.

The observed cross-national differences between China and Canada are attributed to both cultural and structural factors. Even after China has become a HIC, one would expect the purchase behavior of North Americans and Chinese to be still somewhat different. Therefore, marketers are advised to build their COO and brand promotional programs in China differently from those in North America. Advertising messages in China should be emotional rather than cognitive, emphasizing such themes as acceptability of a COO or brand name by other group members (Moore, Harris and Chen 1995).

This research should encourage researchers to replicate studies of COO effects in different HICs, NICs and transitional economies using both technologically simple and complex products, possibly evoking different levels of involvement. It would be interesting to choose HICs, NICs and transitional economies with different market structure problems and levels of technological sophistication. Such studies would permit the estimation of interaction effects between market structure, product category, COO and other information cues. Because the present study was limited to only one NIC in a transitional economy, it should be viewed as raising more questions than providing definitive answers. Hopefully, it will encourage other researchers to examine how the level of structural impediment to marketing action may be a key moderator of COO effects.

REFERENCES

Ahmed, S. A., d'Astous, A. and Mathieu, A. (1995), Influences relatives des lieux de conception et d'assemblage sur la perception des produits. *Canadian Journal of Administrative Sciences*, 12 (3), 210-223.

Anonymous (1996), China. *Globe and Mail*, June 23, B8.

Austin, J. E. (1990), *Managing in Developing Countries*. New York: The Free Press.

Bilkey, W. J. and Ness, E. (1982), Country of Origin Effects on Product Evaluations. *Journal of International Business Studies*, 13, 89-99.

Cateora, P. R. (1996), *International Marketing*. Chicago: Richard P. Irwin.

Chao, P. (1993), Partitioning Country-of-Origin Effects: Consumer Evaluations of a Hybrid Product. *Journal of International Business Studies*, 24 (2), 291-306.

Chao, P. (1995), Review of Product-Country Images : Impact and Role in International Marketing. *Journal of Marketing*, 59 (2), 115.

Cochran, W. G. and Cox, G. M. (1957), *Experimental Designs*. Second edition, New York: John Wiley and Sons.

d'Astous, A., Ahmed, S. A. and El Adraoui, M. (1993), L'influence du pays d'origine des produits sur les évaluations des consommateurs. *Gestion*, 18 (2), 14-21.

Ettenson, R., Kuznetzov, A. and Vetrova, E. (1992), Consumer Decision Making in the Soviet Union: A Conjoint Analysis of Brand Name and Country of Origin Effects. In *Marketing for Europe–Marketing for the Future*. K. G. Grunert and D. Fuglede (eds), Aarhus, Denmark: The Aarhus School of Business, 363-380.

Ford, J. B., Latour, M. S. and Henthorne, T. L. (1995), Perceptions of Marital Roles in Purchase Decision Process. *Journal of the Academy of Marketing Science*, 23 (2), 120-131.

Green, R. T., Leonardi, J. P., Chandon, J. L., Cunningham, I. C. A., Verhage, B. and Strazzieri, A. (1983), Societal Development and Family Purchasing Roles: A Cross-National Study. *Journal of Consumer Research*, 9 (4), 436-442.

Hague, E. and Bahn, K. D. (1996), Exploring the Role of the Situation and Cognitive Type of Individuals on the Impact of Advertising. *Marketing and Research Today*, 24 (2), 72-82.

Harris, R., Garner-Earl, B., Sprick, S. J. and Carroll, C. (1994), Effects of Foreign Product Names and Country-of-Origin Attributions on Advertisement Evaluations. *Psychology and Marketing*, 11 (2), 129-144.

Harvey, M. and Ronkainen, I. (1985), International Counterfeiters: Marketing Success Without the Cost and the Risk. *Columbia Journal of World Business*, 25 (Fall), 37-45.

I.M.F. (1994), *International Financial Statistics*. Washington, D.C.: International Monetary Fund.

Kaynak, E. and Kucukemirglu, O. (1992), Sourcing of Industrial Products: Regiocentric Orientation of Chinese Organizational Buyers. *European Journal of Marketing*, 26 (5), 36-55.

Li, W. K. and Monroe, K. B. (1992), The Role of Country of Origin Information on Buyer's Product Evaluation: An In-Depth Interview Approach. In *Enhancing Knowledge Development*, Vol. 3, Proceedings of the American Marketing Association Educator's Conference, 274-280.

Liping, S., Hanshang, W., Sibin, W. and Shanhua, Y. (1995), Changes in China's Social Structure Following the Reforms. *Social Sciences in China*, 16 (2), 70-80.

Maheswaran, D. (1994), Country of Origin as a Stereotype: Effects of Consumer Expertise and Attribute Strength on Product Evaluation. *Journal of Consumer Research*, 21 (2), 354-365.

Moore, D. J., Harris, W. D. and Chen, F. C. (1995), Affect Intensity: An Individual Difference Response to Advertising Aspects. *Journal of Consumer Research*, 22 (September), 154-164.

Mummulaneni, V., Dubas, K. M. and Chao, C. (1996), Chinese Purchasing Manager's Preference and Trade-offs in Supplier Selection. *Industrial Marketing Management*, 25, 115-124.

Niss, H. (1996), Country of Origin Marketing Over the Product Life Cycle: A Danish Case Study. *European Journal of Marketing*, 30 (3), 6-22.

Osland, G. E. and Cavusgil, S. T. (1996), Performance Issues in U.S.-China Joint Ventures. *California Management Review*, 38 (2), 106-130.

Özsomer, A. and Cavusgil, S. T. (1991), Country-of-Origin Effects on Product Evaluations: A Sequel to the Bilkey and Nes Review. In *Enhancing Knowledge Development in Marketing*, Proceedings of the American Marketing Association Summer Educator's Conference, 269-277.

Papadopoulos, N. and Heslop, L. A. (1993), *Product-Country Images*. New York: International Business Press.

Papadopoulos, N., Heslop, L. A. and Bamossy, G. (1990), A Comparative Image Analysis of Domestic Versus Imported Products. *International Journal of Research in Marketing*, 7 (4), 283-294.

Papadopoulos, N., Heslop, L. A. and Beracs, J. (1990), National Stereotypes and Product Evaluations in a Socialist Country. *International Marketing Review*, 7 (1), 32-47.

Ralston, D. A., Gustafson, D. J., Cheung, F. M. and Terpstra, R. A. (1993), Differences in Managerial Values: A Study of U.S., Hong Kong and P.R.C. Managers. *Journal of International Business Studies*, 24 (2), 249-275.

Ralston, D. A., Gustafson, D. J., Terpstra, R. A. and Holt, D. H. (1995), Pre-Post Tiananmen Square: Changing Values of Chinese Managers. *Asia Pacific Journal of Management*, 12 (1), 1-20.

Roth, M. S. and Romeo, S. B. (1992), Matching Product Category and Country Image Perceptions: A Framework for Managing Country-of-Origin Effects. *Journal of International Business Studies*, 23 (3), 477-497.

Samiee, S. (1994), Consumer Evaluation of Products in a Global Market. *Journal of International Business Studies*, 25 (3), 477-497.

Smith, R. E. and Swinyard, W. R. (1983), Attitude-Behavior Consistency: The Impact of Product Trial vs. Advertising. *Journal of Marketing Research*, 20, 257-267.

Sukhdial, A. S., Chakraborty, G. and Steiger, E. S. (1995), Measuring Values Can Sharpen Segmentation in the Luxury Auto Market. *Journal of Advertising Research*, 35 (1), 9-22.

Thorelli, H. B. (1985), Market Socialism in the People's Republic of China. *International Marketing Review*, 2 (2), 7-14.

Vear, D. (1996a), Reprendre le fil de l'histoire. *Le Devoir*, August 19, 1-8.

Vear, D. (1996b), La chanson française à la conquête de la Chine. *Le Devoir*, August 20, 1-8.

Vernon-Wortzel, H. and Wortzel, L. (1987), The Emergence of Free Market Retailing in the People's Republic of China: Promises and Consequences. *California Management Review*, 29 (3), 59-76.

Xing, F. (1995), The Chinese Cultural System: Implications in Cross-Cultural Management. *SAM Advanced Management System*, 60 (1), 14-20.

Yau, O. (1988), Chinese Cultural Values: Their Dimensions and Marketing Implications. *European Journal of Marketing*, 22 (5), 37-48.

The Effects
of Country-of-Brand and Brand Name
on Product Evaluation and Consideration:
A Cross-Country Comparison

John S. Hulland

SUMMARY. This study investigates the individual effects of brand name and the country-of-brand (COB) on consumers' overall product evaluations when only brand name information is provided. The effects of these same factors on brand consideration (and rejection) are also explored. A study involving subjects from two countries was conducted to test these effects in a cross-cultural context. The results show a strong COB effect despite the lack of available COB information, suggesting that country-of-origin (COO) effects are extremely robust. However, brand name also plays a strong and incremental role in influencing subjects' evaluations. Furthermore, these effects differ by subject nationality. Finally, the results show that COB and brand both have an incremental impact on brand consideration beyond that of brand evaluation. Consequently, COB and brand should both be viewed as important in-

John S. Hulland is Associate Professor and R.A. Barford Professor in Marketing Communication, Ivey Business School, University of Western Ontario, London, Ontario N6A 3K7, Canada (E-mail: jhulland@ivey.uwo.ca).

The author thanks Dave Burgoyne, John Kennedy, Paul Beamish, and the editor and reviewers of the *Journal of International Consumer Marketing* for their helpful comments on earlier drafts of this paper.

The author gratefully acknowledges the financial support provided for this work by the Social Sciences and Humanities Research Council of Canada, the Ivey Business School, and the Barford family.

[Haworth co-indexing entry note]: "The Effects of Country-of-Brand and Brand Name on Product Evaluation and Consideration: A Cross-Country Comparison." Hulland, John S. Co-published simultaneously in *Journal of International Consumer Marketing* (International Business Press, an imprint of The Haworth Press, Inc.) Vol. 11, No. 1, 1999, pp. 23-40; and: *Consumer Behavior in Asia: Issues and Marketing Practice* (ed: T. S. Chan) International Business Press, an imprint of The Haworth Press, Inc., 1999, pp. 23-40. Single or multiple copies of this article are available for a fee from The Haworth Document Delivery Service [1-800-342-9678, 9:00 a.m. - 5:00 p.m. (EST). E-mail address: getinfo@haworthpressinc.com].

puts to consumer decision making, and both must be carefully managed. *[Article copies available for a fee from The Haworth Document Delivery Service: 1-800-342-9678. E-mail address: getinfo@haworthpressinc.com]*

KEYWORDS. Country-of-origin, country-of-brand, product evaluation, Hong Kong, Canada

Many firms have adopted a multiple country strategy for design, manufacturing, and assembly as their operations have become increasingly international in scope. For example, Chrysler shifted some of its assembly operations to Mexico to take advantage of lower wage rates and favorable tariff arrangements. However, functions such as product design and brand management typically remain head office responsibilities. To talk of a single country-of-origin effect then is misleading. Instead, it is useful to think about various more specific aspects of COO (Chao 1993; Ulgado and Lee 1993), including country-of-brand (COB), the country with which an individual brand name is most closely associated.

The current study examines how brand names influence consumer product evaluation and consideration in a cross-country, COO context. Recent research has suggested that both COO and brand information are important to consumers' product evaluations (e.g., Cordell 1992; Han and Terpstra 1988; Hulland, Todiño, and Lecraw 1996; Johansson and Nebenzahl 1986; Nes and Bilkey 1993; Tse and Gorn 1993; Ulgado and Lee 1993). Specifically, the current study examines this issue by providing consumers only with brand name information (and no direct COB information), permitting a very conservative test of the COB effect, and allowing a comparison of the relative importance of brand name and COB information.

The current study is also the first to examine the effects of brand and COB information on product consideration. In a typical purchase situation, consumers are faced with a large number of product alternatives, but only seriously consider a small subset of these for purchase (e.g., see Howard and Sheth 1969; Hulland and Vandenbosch 1996; Lehmann and Pan 1994; Urban, Hulland, and Weinberg 1993). While product consideration is in many cases likely to be related to product evaluation, COB and brand name information may have somewhat different impacts on each of these two distinct constructs. Both are examined here.

Finally, this study investigates differences in consumer product evaluation, consideration, and rejection in two separate countries: Canada and Hong Kong. Although this comparison is more suggestive than definitive, the results found here suggest that there are substantial cross-country differences in the key dependent variables studied.

BACKGROUND AND OBJECTIVES

Brand Evaluation and Brand Consideration (Rejection)

The relationship between brand evaluation and country-of-origin information has been well studied (Papadopoulos and Heslop 1993; Samiee 1994). Most previous studies have examined the effect of COO information on product evaluations (e.g., Erickson, Johansson, and Chao 1984; Han 1989; Hong and Wyer 1989) or hypothetical purchase preferences (e.g., Cordell 1992; Roth and Romero 1992). In contrast, little is known how COO information influences brand consideration (and its conceptual counterpart, brand rejection). The current study seeks to begin to rectify this situation.

The notion of brand consideration was first introduced into marketing as an integral component in the Howard and Sheth (1969) theory of buyer behavior. As defined by Howard (1977), the consideration (or "evoked") set is "the subset of brands that a consumer considers buying out of the set of brands that he or she is aware of in a given product class." Thus, a brand which is considered by the consumer is simply a member of this set, which tends to be quite stable over extended periods of time (Hulland and Vandenbosch 1996; Narayana and Markin 1975; Shocker et al. 1991).

Many researchers have looked at differences in the size of consumers' consideration sets across product categories (e.g., Narayana and Markin 1975; Hauser and Wernerfelt 1990), or have examined the correlation between the consideration set size and a variety of demographic and psychographic variables (e.g., Belonax and Mittelstaedt 1978). However, little previous research has investigated the relationship between COO and brand consideration.

From one perspective, investigation of the relationship between COB and brand consideration may appear to be pointless. Previous research has demonstrated a strong relationship between brand evaluation and brand consideration (e.g., Hauser and Wernerfelt 1990; Roberts and Lattin 1991; Urban et al. 1993). However, Nedungadi (1990) convincingly demonstrated that brand consideration and brand evaluation involve distinct processes, and that they should be viewed as independent constructs (see also Shocker et al. 1991).

Following Narayana and Markin (1975), the "universal set" can be defined as the set of alternatives which are available (or potentially available) to consumers. Typically, a consumer will be aware of some of these alternatives (due to manufacturers' chosen advertising and distribution strategies) and unaware of others. For those alternatives with which the consumer is aware, some will be seriously considered for purchase (i.e., the consideration set), while others will be rejected outright (the "rejection set"). The remaining alternatives with which a consumer is aware form his/her "inert set."

In general, alternatives in the consideration set are evaluated most favorably, whereas alternatives in the rejection set receive the lowest evaluations. Although the processes used by consumers to form their consideration and rejection sets are still not well understood, many researchers believe that extrinsic information cues (such as brand names and COO information) influence their formation. For example, Cordell (1992) suggested that COO information may be most frequently used by consumers "as a screening device to determine whether a product enters the [consumer's] consideration set."

It is generally accepted that extrinsic cues such as price, brand name, and COO information significantly affect consumers' product evaluations (e.g., Bilkey and Nes 1982; Özsomer and Cavusgil 1991). Because evaluation and consideration are often closely related, extrinsic cues should also affect consumers' consideration processes. However, it is not currently clear whether these extrinsic cues have a direct impact on brand consideration (and rejection), or only an indirect impact through their effects on brand evaluation. The potential effects of two such extrinsic cues–COB and brand name information–are explored in the following sections. The potential effect of consumer nationality is also discussed.

Country-of-Origin

Many studies have found that consumers develop country stereotypes on the basis of their social and personal experiences (e.g., Papadopoulos and Heslop 1993; Samiee 1994; Tse and Gorn 1993), and that they prefer to buy their products from some countries over others. For example, Japan has developed a strong reputation for designing and manufacturing superior consumer electronics products (Han and Terpstra 1988; Ulgado and Lee 1993). Consumers' evaluations of products made in different countries have been found to be consistent with this stereotyping explanation (Cordell 1992; Nagashima 1970). Thus, COO (and, more specifically, COB) information should have a significant impact on consumers' evaluations of products from different countries. However, while this direct effect of COB information on consumers' product evaluations will in turn influence their product consideration and rejection processes, there is currently no evidence to suggest that COB information will directly affect either product consideration or rejection.

Brand Name

Many early COO studies focused primarily on the impact that country image has on consumers' evaluative processes. Even when brand names were explicitly included in these studies, the specific effects of individual brand names were often ignored. As noted by Johansson et al. (1985, p. 388): " . . . most studies have involved only a single cue, that is, country-of-origin . . . " This general approach has tended to bias results in favor of finding a significant COO effect.

Recent work has attempted to focus more attention on the interaction between COO and brand name (e.g., Cordell 1992; Han and Terpstra 1988; Hulland et al. 1996; Nes and Bilkey 1993; Tse and Gorn 1993; Ulgado and Lee 1993). Most of these studies have found evidence suggesting that brand name and COO information cues both have an impact on consumers' evaluations, with COO generally playing a more prominent role. In the current study, brand name information is given greater prominence; thus, the relative importance of COB and brand name information is unclear. Nonetheless, both types of information should have a significant impact on consumers' product evaluations.

The likely effects of COB and brand name on product consideration and rejection are less clear. Following the line of reasoning advanced in the previous section, it seems plausible that both COB and brand information will influence product consideration (and rejection) only indirectly through product evaluation.

In addition to these general effects of brand and COB information on evaluation, consideration, and rejection, there are also likely to be important differences between brands. Just as individual countries generate specific–and highly unique–images in consumers' minds, individual brands also often stimulate unique images for many consumers (e.g., see Aaker 1996a; Keller 1993; Park, Jaworski, and MacInnis 1986). Thus, while COB stereotypes may influence consumers' evaluations, there should also be strong differences in evaluations for any given brand name, due to brand image differences.

Consumer Nationality

Previous studies have shown that the COO effect tends to be specific to consumers' own countries (e.g., Nagashima 1970) and to individual consumer traits (e.g., Shimp and Sharma 1987). Although relatively little is known about the systematic effects of these factors on consumers' use of COO information (Heslop and Papadopoulos 1993; Ulgado and Lee 1993), differences in product evaluation, consideration, and rejection can be expected when examining consumer groups from different countries.

RESEARCH METHOD

Subjects

A questionnaire was administered to two groups of undergraduate university student subjects, one in Hong Kong (n = 89) and the other in Canada (n =

68). Subjects were recruited from these two nations for both theoretical and practical reasons. From a theoretical standpoint, U.S. and Japanese consumers might be expected to exhibit strong loyalty for brands from their own countries (cf., Han 1988; Nagashima 1970). In order to permit a more conservative test, subjects from regional neighbor nations (Canada, Hong Kong) were used instead.

Two additional practical concerns guided the choice of Hong Kong as the second nation in the current study. First, for comparative purposes, it was important to survey consumers from a developed Asian country. Second, limited resources precluded translation of the questionnaire into a second language. The Hong Kong subjects surveyed here were familiar with and comfortable using English. A subsequent comparison of the basic demographic information provided by the two groups indicated no significant demographic differences between the two groups in terms of age, gender, or education.

Procedure

Subjects completed the questionnaires at their own pace. Twenty-two different Japanese and U.S. television brand names were included in the study (see Table 1 for a complete list). Subjects were first asked to identify ("yes" or "no") whether or not they recognized, currently owned, or had previously purchased each of these brands. They then provided an overall evaluation for each of the brands they recognized, on a five-point strongly agree/strongly disagree format Likert scale, in response to the statement "This brand is very good overall." They then indicated ("yes" or "no") whether they would "seriously consider" and "never consider" each of the twenty-two brands and provided demographic information. (Other measurement items were also included in the questionnaire, but are not relevant here.) Finally, subjects were told the purpose of the study and given an opportunity to ask questions.

The product category used in the survey was television sets. Previous researchers have found that student subjects find consumer electronic products to be both highly relevant and interesting (e.g., Tse and Gorn 1993). The brands included in the survey represented all major branded alternatives available in both the Canadian and Hong Kong markets. Additional space was available to write in the names of other television brands, but few subjects provided such information, suggesting that the basic set of brands listed was relatively complete.

COB was determined for each brand by identifying the home country for the companies owning these brands. Home countries were assessed by referring to two separate, commercially available brand registries (the *International Directory of Company History* and the *International Trade Names*

TABLE 1. Means: Brand Recognition and Evaluation, by Brand and Subject Nationality

Brand Name	Recognition Proportion			Evaluation			Country of Brand
	Hong Kong	Canada	Total	Hong Kong	Canada	Total	
√ Citizen	.85	.81	.83	2.88	2.51	2.72	Japan
√ Emerson	.40	.81	.57	2.44	2.30	2.38	USA
Funai	.00	.02	.01	—	1.00	1.00	Japan
√ GE	.51	.93	.69	2.81	3.04	2.91	USA
√ Hitachi	.81	.97	.88	2.98	4.30	3.55	Japan
√ JVC	.78	.86	.81	3.66	3.57	3.62	Japan
√ Magnavox	.31	.81	.52	3.12	3.28	3.19	USA
√ Mitsubishi	.80	.78	.79	3.23	3.51	3.35	Japan
√ NEC	.80	.26	.57	3.36	3.48	3.41	Japan
√ Panasonic	.79	.98	.87	3.73	3.98	3.84	Japan
Prism	.00	.12	.05	—	1.40	1.40	USA
Proton	.00	.06	.03	—	2.00	2.00	USA
√ Quasar	.47	.58	.52	2.81	2.44	2.65	USA
√ RCA	.71	.89	.78	3.16	4.31	3.66	USA
Realistic	.00	.71	.31	—	2.29	2.29	USA
√ Sanyo	.84	.90	.86	3.06	3.06	3.06	Japan
√ Sears	.62	.74	.67	2.52	2.61	2.56	USA
√ Sharp	.81	.84	.83	3.71	3.55	3.64	Japan
√ Sony	.75	1.00	.86	3.88	4.73	4.25	Japan
Sylvania	.00	.72	.31	—	2.50	2.50	USA
√ Toshiba	.78	.93	.85	3.62	4.10	3.83	Japan
√ Zenith	.57	.96	.74	2.65	4.50	3.45	USA

√ indicates brands retained for further analysis
Note: Recognition proportion is the aggregate proportion of recognition for the relevent group.
   Evaluation is the average brand evaluation for the group with 1 representing "very bad" brand and 5 a "very good" brand.

Directory). The COB for each of the twenty-two brands used in the study is shown in Table 1. Table 1 also reports the proportion of brand recognition and average brand evaluation, by brand, across all subjects. Because several brands were recognized by only a small subset of subjects, a decision was made to retain only those brands with which at least fifty percent of the subjects were familiar. These brands are indicated with a check mark in Table 1 (i.e., seven U.S.-based brands and ten Japan-based brands).

RESULTS

Brand Evaluation

To examine the relative impacts of COB and brand name information, as well as subject nationality, on overall evaluation, an ANOVA model was employed. Two levels for COB and subject nationality were used, along with 16 levels for brand. An interaction term between COB and nationality was also included. Results from this model are presented in Table 2. Clearly, COB, subject nationality, brand name, and the COB-subject nationality interaction all had a significant effect on overall evaluation.

The Canadian subjects generally rated all brands higher than did their Hong Kong counterparts. Furthermore, on average Japanese brands were rated more highly than U.S. brands. The significant interaction observed here resulted from the following: both Hong Kong and Canadian subjects rated Japanese brands quite favorably; in contrast, Canadian subjects rated U.S. brands far more favorably than did Hong Kong subjects.

The relative importance of the COB and brand name cues can be tested formally by using a variance ratio test. Under the null hypothesis (i.e., both factors are equally important), the variance ratio (VR = MS(COB)/MS(Brand)) is distributed F(df(COB), df(Brand)). In the present case, VR = 1.80 has a distribution F(1,15), which does not differ significantly from a value of 1. Thus, although Table 2 suggests that COB had a bigger impact than brand name on product evaluation, statistically they have equivalent effects.

Brand Consideration and Rejection

Table 3 reports the average probability of brand consideration and brand rejection for each brand in the study, by COB and subject nationality. Table 3

TABLE 2. ANOVA Results: Overall Evaluation as a Function of COB, Subject Nationality, and Brand

Variable	SS	DF	MS	F	Significance of F
COB	28.4	1	28.4	25.8	.000
Nationality	25.3	1	25.3	23.1	.000
Brand	237.7	15	15.8	14.4	.000
COB × nationality	8.5	1	8.5	7.8	.000
Within cells	1390	1267	1.1		

TABLE 3. Brand Consideration and Rejection, by Brand and Subject Nationality

Brand Name	Consideration			Rejection		
	Hong Kong	Canada	Difference	Hong Kong	Canada	Difference
Citizen	0.09	0.05	0.04	0.39	0.40	−0.01
Emerson	0.00	0.02	−0.02	0.60	0.40	*0.20*
GE	0.04	0.11	−0.07	0.50	0.43	0.07
Hitachi	0.26	0.30	−0.04	0.07	0.09	−0.02
JVC	0.51	0.41	0.10	0.03	0.06	−0.03
Magnavox	0.04	0.25	*−0.21*	0.48	0.11	*0.37*
Mitsubishi	0.26	0.37	*−0.11*	0.15	0.11	0.04
NEC	0.33	0.27	0.06	0.12	0.23	*−0.11*
Panasonic	0.83	0.56	*0.27*	0.03	0.12	−0.09
Quasar	0.08	0.00	0.08	0.46	0.42	0.04
RCA	0.20	0.59	*−0.39*	0.45	0.07	*0.38*
Sanyo	0.03	0.25	*−0.23*	0.19	0.29	−0.10
Sears	0.05	0.11	−0.06	0.49	0.43	0.06
Sharp	0.35	0.32	0.03	0.15	0.11	0.04
Sony	0.85	0.97	*−0.12*	0.00	0.00	0.00
Toshiba	0.52	0.50	0.02	0.06	0.05	0.01
Zenith	0.13	0.44	*−0.31*	0.53	0.11	*0.42*

Note: Differences greater than 10 percent in absolute magnitude are noted in bold and italicized.

also reports differences in the Hong Kong and Canadian subjects' probabilities. Clearly, Hong Kong subjects are less inclined to consider brands in general, and more inclined to reject them.

To examine the effects of COB, brand name, subject nationality, and product evaluation on product consideration and rejection, models using binomial logit analysis (Ben-Akiva and Lerman 1985) were estimated. Use of logit analysis is necessary in this case because the dependent variables (brand consideration, brand rejection) are dichotomous. Separate logit models were constructed for brand consideration and brand rejection, using overall brand evaluation, COB, subject nationality, an interaction between COB and nationality, and dummy variables representing the individual brands as independent variables. Dummy variables for the Toshiba and Zenith brands were not included in these models, since their effects are already included in the constant and interaction terms.

Results for these two models are reported in Table 4. Both models are

TABLE 4. Brand Consideration and Rejection: Logit Results

Variable	Consideration[a]		Rejection	
Overall brand evaluation	0.90	(0.06)***	−0.97	(0.08)***
Nationality (Canada = 1)	−0.25	(0.09)**	0.07	(0.13)
Country of brand (US = 1)	−1.09	(0.36)**	3.34	(0.78)***
Nationality × COB	0.45	(0.18)*	−0.39	(0.18)*
Brand dummies:				
Citizen	−2.31	(0.41)***	3.13	(0.76)***
Emerson	−2.96	(1.04)**	0.97	(0.38)*
GE	−1.09	(0.41)**	0.19	(0.36)
Hitachi	−0.80	(0.28)**	1.02	(0.84)
JVC	−0.06	(0.29)	0.76	(0.87)
Magnavox	−0.39	(0.35)	−0.51	(0.39)
Mitsubishi	−0.36	(0.29)	0.99	(0.84)
NEC	−0.18	(0.32)	1.69	(0.81)*
Panasonic	0.62	(0.29)*	1.15	(0.82)
Quasar	−1.56	(0.48)**	0.30	(0.39)
RCA	0.07	(0.30)	0.40	(0.34)
Sanyo	−2.61	(0.41)***	2.33	(0.76)**
Sears	−1.74	(0.52)***	0.51	(0.35)
Sharp	−0.77	(0.29)**	2.27	(0.78)**
Sony	1.71	(0.18)***	−4.88	(7.41)
Constant	−2.86	(0.33)***	−0.85	(0.76)
Model χ^2 (df = 19)	828, $p < 0.0001$		613, $p < 0.0001$	
Hit rate	79%		84%	
ρ^2	0.336		0.333	
N	1836		1836	

[a] Entries in this table show coefficient estimates and associated standard error terms.
 * $p < 0.05$
 ** $p < 0.01$
 *** $p < 0.001$

highly significant, as indicated by the chi-square, hit rate, and rho-square statistics. Hit rate represents the degree to which the estimated model correctly predicts the observed data. Rho-square roughly corresponds to the R^2 value obtained from regression analysis, but tends to be lower in value (see Ben-Akiva and Lerman 1985).

In the case of brand consideration, overall brand evaluation not surprisingly has a strong and positive impact. More significantly, however, even after the effect of brand evaluation is taken into account, the main effects of subject nationality and COB, and the interaction between the two variables all remain significant. Thus, these factors have a direct effect on both consideration and rejection, as well as an indirect effect through evaluation.

As Table 4 shows, the coefficient on the COB variable is significantly negative, indicating that subjects were generally less likely to consider U.S. brands, and more likely to consider Japanese brands. COB information is apparently being used by subjects to "screen" a limited set of alternatives into their consideration sets. Similarly, the brand rejection results indicate that COB has a significant impact on brand rejection. Subjects were consistently more likely to reject a U.S. brand than a Japanese brand.

Any individual brand can be seriously considered, rejected outright, or neither considered nor rejected (i.e., the consumer is indifferent). The binomial logit model results reported here indicate that COB and subject nationality are used to screen alternatives into both the consideration and rejection sets. Canadian and Hong Kong subjects are both more likely to consider Japanese brands than U.S. brands, but Canadian subjects are more likely than the Hong Kong subjects to consider U.S. brands. A similar (but reversed) pattern of results is found for brand rejection.

Before turning to a more general discussion of these results, it is worth noting that a number of the dummy variables representing individual brands in the binomial logit models differ significantly from zero. To interpret these results, it is important to keep in mind that the brand-specific coefficients differ significantly from zero *after* the effects of brand evaluation, subject nationality, and COB are taken into account. For example, the coefficient for the Citizen brand is significantly negative in the brand consideration model, and significantly positive in the brand rejection model. By way of contrast, the coefficient for Sony is significantly positive in the brand consideration model, and negative (although not significantly so) in the brand rejection model. The implications of these non-zero coefficients are explored further below.

DISCUSSION

Brand Evaluation

The preceding results add to our existing understanding of the country-of-brand (and, by extension, the country-of-origin) phenomenon in a number of ways. First, the country-of-brand was found to have a significant impact on individuals' overall evaluations despite the complete absence of externally available COB information. Consequently, the COB effect observed in this study is completely memory-based. While many previous studies have found strong evidence of a COO effect, they have generally used salient, externally available COO information cues. In a number of extreme cases, COO information was the *only* external cue provided to subjects, potentially biasing findings in favor of a significant COO effect (Han and Terpstra 1988; Johansson et al. 1985). However, the current results suggest that this bias may be less extreme than previously thought.

There are several possible explanations for this finding. For example, COB information is probably very salient to consumers. Papadopoulos (1993) has argued that COB cues are not restricted to "made in" labels on packages, but can take many forms, including brand names which either directly identify the COB or indirectly do so through memory-based associations to the COB, logos and package designs, and associations created via advertising.

A second key finding of the current study is that COB and brand name both appear to have a strong impact on consumers' product evaluations. Furthermore, COB is at least as important as brand, a result consistent with many previous studies (e.g., Han and Terpstra 1988; Tse and Gorn 1993). On the other hand, the evidence here suggests that individual brand names play an important independent role in influencing consumers' evaluations beyond the effect of COB information.

Third, subjects' evaluations were observed to vary systematically by subject nationality in the current study, tending to reflect regional patriotism and/or closer cultural, political, and social affinity between the COB and the consumer's own country. Such results are consistent with findings from a limited number of related previous studies (e.g., Heslop and Papadopoulos 1993; Shimp and Sharma 1987).

Brand Consideration and Rejection

Both brand consideration and brand rejection were influenced directly by COB in the current study. These results are consistent with the suggestion by Cordell (1992) that COO might be used by consumers to "screen" alternatives into their consideration sets, although more work is obviously needed before a definitive statement about the underlying processes can properly be made. However, they also suggest the need for separate and independent studies of the effect of COO information on consumers' consideration (and rejection).

Second, brand consideration and rejection varied systematically by subject nationality. In particular, the Hong Kong subjects were less likely than the Canadian subjects to consider (and more likely to reject) any individual brand. This may be a consequence, at least in part, of Asian consumers' widespread recognition of prestige brands. It may also reflect national (or regional) cultural differences (Hofstede 1983) across the two countries.

A third finding which emerges from the current study is the incremental impact that some brands have on brand consideration and rejection beyond the effects of COB, subject nationality, and overall evaluation. One way of interpreting these incremental effects is to think of them as measures of brand name strength, or brand equity (e.g., Aaker 1996b; Keller 1993). Brands with positive equity (e.g., Sony) tend to be considered more frequently for purchase (and rejected outright less frequently), while the reverse is true for brands with negative equity (e.g., Citizen). Interestingly, some brands are strongly evaluated by both groups (e.g., Sony), some appear to have only regional appeal (e.g., RCA, Panasonic), and some are rejected by all (e.g., Emerson, Quasar).

Managerial Implications

Three major managerial implications emerge from the preceding discussion. First, the results obtained here suggest that overcoming a negative COB bias in the minds of consumers may be extremely difficult. Attempts to modify consumers' evaluations by simple shifts in manufacturing or assembly location may therefore fail. This finding is consistent with the results of recent work by Tse and Lee (1993), which showed that information about a product's component and assembly origins played only a small role in influencing consumers' evaluations. Indeed, once a brand name is linked to a particular COB, it may be very difficult to subsequently shift consumers' perceptions. This will be particularly true if the brand name is well known. For example, Disney, Levi's, and Coca-Cola are all clearly established in the minds of consumers around the world as U.S. brands, regardless of where they are produced and sold. As a result, the link between COB and brand name deserves far greater attention than it has received to date.

Second, managers can have an impact on consumers' processing of brand information in a number of different ways. By increasing advertising expenditures, improving advertising message quality, and expanding distribution, managers can enhance consumer awareness of their brands, an obvious first step to generating sales. However, the current results suggest that *both* COB and brand image need to be managed carefully in order to increase the likelihood of consumer brand consideration (and to avoid brand rejection). Money spent on maintaining or enhancing brand image, while effective in influencing consumers' brand evaluations, may have a considerably smaller impact on their brand consideration. Since other factors (such as COB and subject nationality) can influence brand consideration beyond the effect of overall brand evaluation, marketers should be prepared to learn more about consumers' consideration processes.

Finally, the brand equity measures described earlier are reflective of the strength of individual brands after the effects of subject nationality and COB are taken into account, and thus reflect the pan-national strengths or weaknesses of individual brands. While the approach used here needs further refinement, it may be useful to researchers and managers interested in studying international or global branding questions such as why some brands have stronger pan-national equities than others, or how international/global brands can be managed more effectively. For example, Sony and Citizen are both Japan-based brand names, yet the former does well with both groups in our study and the latter does poorly.

Implications for Future Research

The current findings also suggest directions for future research work. For example, this is the first study to explicitly examine the impact of COB on individuals' brand consideration and rejection assessments. Brand consideration has recently received increased attention by marketers in general (e.g., Hauser and Wernerfelt 1990; Hulland and Vandenbosch 1996; Nedungadi 1990; Roberts and Lattin 1991; Urban et al. 1993), but this interest has not been duplicated in the international marketing area.

Our results also reinforce the need for systematic research into the effects of brand and COO information on consumers' evaluations and choices. Typical studies have either ignored brand information, or have tended to confound brand name and COO. By varying the salience of information within a single study, researchers may be able to untangle the individual effects of COO (or COB) and brand.

Study Limitations

The preceding results and discussion must, of course, be tempered by a recognition of the limitations of the current study. Only two nations were examined, reducing the generalizability of the study's results. As Clark (1990) has noted, we need to develop better cross-national theories if we hope to get beyond the idiosyncrasies of individual studies. Furthermore, only one product category (televisions) was investigated. While similar results might be expected for consumer electronics in general, the approach here needs to be applied to a variety of different products before generalizations can be made.

The use of student subjects may further limit the usefulness of these findings. On the other hand, student subjects are acceptable when tests of theory rather than effect size estimates are the goal. The current paper's focus on theory testing may therefore mitigate this concern. In addition, a recent meta-analysis of the COO literature by Liefeld (1993) found no significant differences between students and other respondents in their influence on COO effect sizes, suggesting that concerns about student subjects may be overstated. Finally, many of our subjects (from both nations) owned their own television set or had participated in the purchase of a set in the recent past. Consequently, for this product category, use of student subjects probably does not compromise external validity.

A different type of concern results from the fact that COB information was neither provided nor measured directly here. Instead, COB was defined as the country most closely associated with registry of the brand. However, not all consumers will correctly identify each individual brand with its corresponding COB. For example (as one reviewer noted), many consumers may believe that Citizen, Panasonic, and perhaps even JVC and NEC are U.S. rather than Japanese brands. The absence of information about individual consumers' perceptions of COB makes it impossible to correct for this. Note, however, that the effects described here indicate the importance of COB *in addition* to brand evaluation (and brand consideration), even when brand name was the only extrinsic cue provided to subjects. Thus, COB adds explanatory power to our models *despite* the potential confound introduced by consumer misperception.

CONCLUSION

The study described in this paper investigated the relationship between COB and brand from a different perspective than previous studies, placing a much increased emphasis on brand name information. Despite the absence of explicit COB information, however, the COB effect was found to have a significant impact on overall product evaluations, suggesting that the COB (and, by extension, COO) effect is extremely robust.

Futhermore, the paper provides an initial exploration of the role played by COB in influencing brand consideration and rejection. The finding that COB information can affect brand consideration (and rejection) beyond its impact on brand evaluation is provocative, but its final interpretation must await our better understanding of the inter-relationships between COB, brand name, evaluation, and consideration.

These findings are broadly consistent with those of other recent studies which have attempted to assess the relative importance of COO and brand information in consumer evaluation and choice. Many of these studies have found evidence that both brand and COO information cues are important (e.g., Han and Terpstra 1988; Hulland et al. 1996; Nes and Bilkey 1993; Tse and Gorn 1993; Wall et al. 1991). Brand name, like country-of-origin, is typically an extrinsic cue which consumers can use to assess the value of a particular product. Presumably, a strong brand gives consumers greater confidence that product quality had been maintained regardless of where the product was manufactured. However, the current study also reconfirms the importance of COO information even when it is not explicitly available at the moment of evaluation (or choice).

REFERENCES

Aaker, David A. *Building Strong Brands*, New York: The Free Press. 1996a.

Aaker, David A. "Measuring Brand Equity Across Products and Markets." *California Management Review* 38 (Spring 1996b): 102-120.

Belonax, Joseph A., and Robert A. Mittelstaedt. "Evoked Set Size as a Function of Number of Choice Criterion and Information Variability." In *Advances in Consumer Research* 5 (1978): 48-51.

Ben-Akiva, Moshe, and Steven R. Lerman. *Discrete Choice Analysis: Theory and Application to Travel Demand*. Cambridge, MA: The MIT Press, 1985.

Bilkey, Warren and Erik Nes. "Country-of-origin Effects on Product Evaluations." *Journal of International Business Studies*, 13 (1982): 89-99.

Chao, Paul. "Partitioning Country of Origin Effects: Consumer Evaluations of a Hybrid Product." *Journal of International Business Studies*, 24 (1993): 291-306.

Clark, Terry. "International Marketing and National Character: A Review and Proposal for an Integrative Theory." *Journal of Marketing* 54 (October 1990): 66-77.

Cordell, Victor V. "Effects of Consumer Preferences for Foreign Sourced Products." *Journal of International Business Studies* 23, no. 2 (1992): 251-269.

Erickson, Gary, Johnny Johansson, and Paul Chao. "Image Variables in Multi-attribute Product Evaluations: Country-of-Origin Effects." *Journal of Consumer Research*, 11, 2 (Sept. 1984): 694-699.

Han, C. Min, and Vern Terpstra. "Country-of-Origin Effects for Uni-National and Bi-National Products." *Journal of International Business Studies* (Summer 1988): 235-255.

Han, C. Min. "Country Image: Halo or Summary Construct." *Journal of Marketing Research*, 26 (1989): 222-229.

Hauser, John R., and Birger Wernerfelt. "An Evaluation Cost Model of Consideration Sets." *Journal of Consumer Research* 16 (March 1990): 393-408.

Heslop, Louise A., and Nicolas Papadopoulos. "'But Who Knows Where or When': Reflections on the Images of Countries and Their Products." In N. Papadopoulos and L. Heslop (eds), *Product and Country Images: Impact and Role in International Marketing*, New York: The Haworth Press, Inc., 1993.

Hofstede, Geert. "The Cultural Relativity of Organizational Practices and Theories." *Journal of International Business Studies* no. 2 (1983): 75-89.

Hong, Sung-Tai, and Robert Wyer, Jr. "Effects of Country-of-Origin and Product Attribute Information on Product Evaluation: An Information Processing Perspective." *Journal of Consumer Research*, 16 (Sept. 1989): 175-187.

Howard, John A. *Consumer Behavior: Application of Theory*. New York: McGraw-Hill, 1977.

Howard, John A., and Jagdish Sheth. *The Theory of Buyer Behavior.* New York: Wiley, 1969.

Hulland, John, and Mark Vandenbosch. "Estimating Choice Models in Data-Sparse Environments: Taking Advantage of Perceived Similarity." *Marketing Letters* 7, no. 4 (1996), 329-339.

Hulland, John, Honorio S. Todiño, Jr., and Donald J. Lecraw. "Country-of-Origin Effects on Sellers' Price Premiums in Competitive Philippine Markets." *Journal of International Marketing* 4, no. 1 (1996): 57-79.

International Directory of Company History. Chicago, IL: St. James Press, 1990.

International Trade Names Directory: Company Index. Detroit, MI: Gale Research Inc., 1988-1989.

Johansson, J.K., S.P. Douglas, and I. Nonaka. "Assessing the Impact of Country of Origin on Product Evaluations." *Journal of Marketing Research* (November 1985): 388-396.

Johansson, Johnny and Isreal Nebenzahl. "Multinational Production: Effect on Brand Value." *Journal of International Business Studies* (Fall 1986): 101-126.

Keller, Kevin L. "Conceptualizing, Measuring, and Managing Customer-Based Brand Equity." *Journal of Marketing* (January, 1993): 1-22.

Liefeld, John. "Experiments on Country-of-Origin Effects: Review and Meta-Analysis of Effect Size." In N. Papadopoulos and L. Heslop (eds), *Product and Country Images: Impact and Role in International Marketing,* New York: The Haworth Press, Inc., 1993.

Nagashimi, Akira. "A Comparison of Japanese and U.S. Attitudes Towards Foreign Products." *Journal of Marketing* (January 1970): 68-74.

Narayana, Chem L., and Rom J. Markin. "Consumer Behavior and Product Performance: An Alternative Conceptualization." *Journal of Marketing* 39 (October 1975): 1-6.

Nedungadi, Prakash. "Recall and Consumer Consideration Sets: Influencing Choice without Altering Brand Evaluation." *Journal of Consumer Research* 17 (December 1990): 263-276.

Nes, Erik and Warren Bilkey. "A Multi-Cue Test of Country-of-Origin Theory." In N. Papadopoulos and L. Heslop (eds), *Product and Country Images: Impact and Role in International Marketing,* New York: The Haworth Press, Inc., 1993.

Özsomer, Aysegul, and S. Tamer Cavusgil. "Country-of-Origin Effects on Product Evaluations: A Sequel to Bilkey and Nes Review." In Mary C. Gilly and F. Robert Dwyer, (eds.), *Enhancing Knowledge Development in Marketing, Volume 2.* Chicago, IL: American Marketing Association (Summer 1991): 269-277.

Papadopoulos, Nicolas. "What Product and Country Images Are and Are Not." In N. Papadopoulos and L. Heslop (eds), *Product and Country Images: Impact and Role in International Marketing,* New York: The Haworth Press, Inc., 1993.

Papadopoulos, Nicolas and Louise Heslop. *Product and Country Images: Impact and Role in International Marketing,* New York: The Haworth Press, Inc., 1993.

Park, C. Whan, Bernard J. Jaworski, and Deborah J. MacInnis. "Strategic Brand Concept-Image Management." *Journal of Marketing* 50 (October 1986): 135-145.

Roberts, John H., and James M. Lattin. "Developing and Testing of a Model of Consideration Set Composition." *Journal of Marketing Research* 28 (November 1991): 429-440.

Roth, Martin, and Jean Romeo. "Matching Product Category and Country Image Perceptions: A Framework for Managing Country-of-Origin Effects." *Journal of International Business Studies*, 23, 3 (1992): 477-497.

Samiee, Saeed. "Customer Evaluation of Products in a Global Market." *Journal of International Business Studies* 25, no. 3 (1994): 579-604.

Shimp, Terence A., and Subhash Sharma. "Consumer Ethnocentrism: Construction and Validation of the CETSCALE." *Journal of Marketing Research* (August 1987): 280-289.

Shocker, Allan D., Moshe Ben-Akiva, Bruno Boccara, and Prakash Nedungadi. "Consideration Set Influences on Consumer Decision-Making and Choice: Issues, Models, and Suggestions." *Marketing Letters* no. 3 (1991): 181-197.

Tse, David K., and Gerald J. Gorn. "An Experiment on the Salience of Country-of-Origin in the Era of Global Brands." *Journal of International Marketing* 1, no. 1 (1993): 57-76.

Tse, David K., and Wei-na Lee. "Removing Negative Country Images: Effects of Decomposition, Branding, and Product Experience." *Journal of International Marketing* 1, no. 4 (1993): 25-48.

Ulgado, Francis M., and Moonkyu Lee. "Consumer Evaluations of Bi-National Products in the Global Market." *Journal of International Marketing* 1, no. 3 (1993): 5-22.

Urban, Glen L., John S. Hulland, and Bruce D. Weinberg. "Premarket Forecasting for New Consumer Durable Goods: Modeling Categorization, Elimination, and Consideration Phenomena." *Journal of Marketing* 57 (April 1993): 47-63.

Communicating with *the* Cohort: Exploring Generation X$^{ASIA'S}$ Attitudes Towards Advertising

Michael T. Ewing
Albert Caruana

SUMMARY. Rapidly changing demography, coupled with unprecedented economic growth, make Southeast Asia a particularly important target market. Representing almost a quarter of all Asian consumers, 20-to-30 year-olds are attracting considerable attention from both MNCs and regional marketers. What makes this segment particularly interesting is their real and perceived values and orientations towards marketing. Labeled 'Generation X' in North America and elsewhere, popular belief is that 20-to-30 year-olds are generally cynical, pessimistic and 'anti-advertising.' This stereotype has to some degree found its way into Asia. This study sets out to investigate the validity of the Generation X proposition in Asia, and to shed some light on Asian Xers and their attitudes towards advertising. *[Article copies available for a fee from The Haworth Document Delivery Service: 1-800-342-9678. E-mail address: getinfo@haworthpressinc.com]*

KEYWORDS. Generation X, consumer attitudes, advertising, Singapore, Malaysia, Hong Kong

---

Michael T. Ewing is Lecturer, School of Marketing, Curtin Business School, Perth, Western Australia. Albert Caruana is Senior Lecturer, Department of Marketing, University of Malta.

Address correspondence to: Michael T. Ewing, School of Marketing, Curtin Business School, GPO Box U1987, Perth, 6001, Western Australia (E-mail: ewingm@cbs.curtin.edu.au).

[Haworth co-indexing entry note]: "Communicating with *the* Cohort: Exploring Generation X$^{ASIA'S}$ Attitudes Towards Advertising." Ewing, Michael T., and Albert Caruana. Co-published simultaneously in *Journal of International Consumer Marketing* (International Business Press, an imprint of The Haworth Press, Inc.) Vol. 11, No. 1, 1999, pp. 41-53; and: *Consumer Behavior in Asia: Issues and Marketing Practice* (ed: T. S. Chan) International Business Press, an imprint of The Haworth Press, Inc., 1999, pp. 41-53. Single or multiple copies of this article are available for a fee from The Haworth Document Delivery Service [1-800-342-9678, 9:00 a.m. - 5:00 p.m. (EST). E-mail address: getinfo@haworthpressinc.com].

INTRODUCTION

After decades of being targeted, researched and advertised to, baby boomers are no longer the marketing *group du jour* they once were. A new segment has emerged. While not as large as their predecessors, they are nevertheless a particularly important demographic target market. In North America the cohort has been labeled 'Generation X,' and elsewhere as the 'MTV Generation, the Pepsi Generation, Slackers, (Baby) Busters, Posties, Twenty-somethings' and the 'Brat Pack.' Regardless of description, this new generation of consumers represent a challenging opportunity for global marketers.

Generation Xers, a moniker coined by post-boom American pop art author Douglas Coupland (1991) represent approximately 21% of the world's population. In the nine Asian market-oriented economies (including Vietnam), the segment comprises some 87 million, and if China is included, 350 million (Ewing and Pascual, 1997). No age cohort in history has received more media attention than the so-called *X Generation* (Shimp, 1997). Scholarly treatment of the generation has identified it as Americans born between 1961 and 1981 (Strauss and Howe, 1991), an age band which has subsequently been narrowed to include those born between 1965 and 1978 (Shimp, 1997). Generation X is the smallest generation of adults to appear in the US since the 1950s and the first generation in recent times to be smaller than the one before it. It is predicted that this trend will continue, at least to the turn of the century (Johnson, 1996).

ADVERTISING TO GENERATION X

While the cohort's buying power is substantial (Appelbaum, 1992; Schiffman and Kanuk, 1994), their collective attitude towards traditional media advertising, and television in particular, ranges from moderately skeptical to vehemently cynical (Leo, 1993). However, with retailing becoming more and more competitive, manufacturers and merchants alike are going to extreme lengths to appeal to this new generation. For the most part, Generation Xers appear completely uninterested in marketing appeals targeted specifically at them (Donaton, 1993). In particular, they reject stereotypical portrayals of themselves as 'young and foolish' (Freeman, 1995; Harrington, 1995). Notwithstanding, more and more companies are making concerted efforts to communicate with the cohort. Manufacturers of softdrinks [Pepsi] (Jensen, 1996), beer [Budweiser] (Rubel, 1996), autos [Toyota RAV4, BMW, Chrysler Neon] (Freeman, 1996; McCarthy and Parpis, 1995; DeCoursey, 1996), cosmetics [Liz Claiborne] (Verzone, 1996), cameras [Polaroid] (Houghton, 1997) and even life insurers (West, 1995) are actively appealing to Xers, with varying degrees of success.

In addition to their general disdain towards advertising (TV advertising in particular), Xers' media habits are substantially different to those of their baby-boomer parents. Xers are generally opposed to the persuasive influence of television (Macalister, 1994). In fact, 18-29 year-old Americans watch less television overall than any other group (Stipp, 1994). Rather, they are more inclined to read niche magazines targeted specifically at them (Huhn, 1994; Adams, 1996; Jensen, 1994), or written by Xers for Xers (Isler, 1994). In fact, Ritchie (1995) concludes that in addition to being extremely sophisticated media consumers, Xers favor a variety of media and advertisers will have to experiment with different media vehicles (in Freeman, 1995). Marketers waiting to tap the tremendous potential of the segment need to distinguish between two key aspects of any young person's identity: the generation to which they truly belong and the simple fact that they are young (Ritchie, 1992).

GENERATION X^ASIA

To date the overwhelming majority of literature on Generation X has been written from a North American perspective. Assuming that each generation is a product of the times, an examination of the American times that brought about Generation X is not paralleled in Asia (Ewing and Pascual, 1997). For example, in her examination of Singaporean Xers, Chang (1996) concludes that the island's 20-to-30 year-olds have extraordinarily high expectations in terms of career progression, remuneration, material possessions (the 'Singapore Dream' of owning private property and a car), and are considerably less job-loyal than their parents. In fact, there have been few socioeconomic parallels between the two regions in recent years. In an analysis of 10 Asian countries, Ewing and Pascual (1997) found that 20- to 29-year-old Asians share a wide variety of characteristics that differentiate them from their respective (national) populations at large. These differences were most pronounced in terms of media habits, hobbies and pastimes, tastes in clothing, food, travel destinations and music. Unlike the US, where Xers are reportedly less brand loyal, Asian 'twenty-somethings' are just as brand loyal as their parents' generation. In fact, one of the most outstanding differences between Asian Xers and their North American counterparts is the former's voraciousness in availing of market options. But perhaps the most noteworthy characteristic of Asian Xers, from the perspective of this study, is their relative media receptivity. They are not nearly as mass media averse as American Xers, and are indeed a generation cultivated on a global communications culture: satellite television, internet surfing, virtual shopping–consumers who are truly 'wired' to the global village (Ewing and Pascual, 1997). The notion of an Asian Xer is not confined to the more developed countries like Hong

Kong and Singapore. Preliminary work in China by Ariga and his colleagues describe a 'Generation III' (18-to-29 year-olds) as having a 'good educational background and blessed with a good aspect of the market economy systems that promises a brighter future for people who earn enough money' (Ariga, Yasue and Gu, 1997, p. 21). Furthermore, they found that Chinese Xers are attracted towards big brand names, have a 'cut-above-the-rest' mentality and fall into the 'newer the better' syndrome–all characteristics that send positive signals to marketing communicators in the region.

STUDY OBJECTIVES

A basic tenant of the Generation X stereotype is their apparent cynicism towards advertising and the media. Ritchie (1995) holds that 'no icon and certainly no commercial is safe from their (Xers') irony, their sarcasm or their remote control.' These, according to Ritchie, are the tools with which Generation X keeps the world in perspective. More recently, those studying the cohort and their media habits have begun to acknowledge the fact that direct comparisons between Xers and Boomers cannot be made because of the vastly different environments in which they have been exposed to, and consume media. Xers spent a good deal of their childhood in front of a TV screen (Holtz, 1995), and this exposure may have provided them with the 'media savvy' to avoid being influenced by advertising, as well as bringing a certain 'connoisseurship' to their appreciation of advertising (Thau, 1996). This study seeks therefore to provide empirical evidence of (Asian) Xers' attitudes towards advertising. In this regard, the cohort's overall attitudes will be investigated, as well as their attitudes towards both the *institution* and the *practice* of advertising. The present study is an extension (but not a replication) of Mittal's (1994) study of North American public assessment of TV advertising. The study builds on a stream of prior research on attitudes towards advertising, most of which focused on TV advertising specifically (see for example, Aaker and Bruzzone, 1981, 1985; Biel and Bridgewater, 1990; Schlinger, 1979). In investigating the *institution* of advertising, the study incorporates the exploratory research by Mittal and Pollay, as well as earlier work by Gossage (1986), Kirkpatrick (1986) and Ogilvy (1983). A secondary objective of the study focuses on whether differences in culture, industrial development, marketing orientation and scope and influence of advertising among the three countries will result in significant differences in attitudes.

METHODOLOGY

Data for the study were collected in Singapore, Malaysia and Hong Kong: with 57, 106 and 43 useable surveys analyzed respectively. Respondents were primarily students aged between 17 and 30. Thirty-three percent of respondents were male, and all between the ages of 17 and 30. Specific sample demographics are reported in Table 1.

It is important to point out that at least one sample bias may be noted. The sample is skewed towards higher levels of education, and earlier works by Bauer and Greyser (1968) and Mittal (1994) suggest that higher education is associated with somewhat less favorable attitudes towards advertising. However, as Light (1990) points out, *this* is the age of the smarter generation, where consumers will be even more demanding, more educated, more informed, and more skeptical than ever before. In analyzing the results of the study, use was made of Analysis of Variance techniques (ANOVA ONE-WAY), and limited use of Chi-squared testing in order to assess the statistical significance of observed differences. Many of the findings pointed to overall similarities between the three populations examined, with some quite small but statistically significant differences superimposed. Here the concern might be "Type II" errors: failure to recognize real differences. A larger sample would have increased the power of the tests applied, possibly increasing the incidence of significant differences. Nevertheless, it is important to stress that statistical significance should not be confused with substantive importance. Any differences *worthy of attention* will be revealed by the research design applied in this paper.

RESULTS

Contrary to 'Western logic' expressed primarily through North American sentiments towards Xers, the research confirmed an overall positive attitude towards advertising in general. The overwhelming majority (85%) of respondents consider advertising to be at least somewhat essential. Similarly, most respondents report advertising to be either quite or very important to

TABLE 1. Sample Demographics

Demographic	Singapore	Malaysia	Hong Kong
Gender			
Males	17	37	13
Females	40	69	30
Age			
17-20	3	66	4
21-25	39	38	19
26-30	15	2	20

them. In terms of their overall evaluation of the institution of advertising, a third remain undecided, while two-thirds consider it good. Lastly, half of the respondents reported to like advertising, which given the plethora of literature highlighting the importance of likability in advertising, is indeed a significant and considerably positive revelation for Asian marketers (Table 2).

Following the broad guidelines suggested by Mittal (1994) and Pollay and Mittal (1993), this study sought to investigate Asian Xers' perceptions regarding the consequences of advertising. This particular focus seemed pertinent given Xers' apparent disdain of both marketers and their advertising attempts (Leo, 1993; Freeman, 1995). A total of 29 statements reflecting beliefs about advertising's desirable and undesirable consequences were explored, and are arranged under 10 broad headings in Table 3.

On a scale of 1 to 7, respondents generally considered advertising a valuable source of marketplace information (mean = 4.95), particularly in terms of keeping them up-to-date on product availability (mean = 5.61). While respondents' confidence in advertised brands/products was not particularly

TABLE 2. General Opinions on Advertising

	Singapore	Malaysia	Hong Kong
Q. Do you consider advertising:			
Not essential at all	1	0	1
Somewhat essential	5	16	7
Quite essential	29	43	23
Very essential	21	47	12
Q. To me, advertising is:			
Not at all important	0	1	1
Somewhat important	9	26	16
Quite important	31	43	20
Very important	17	36	7
Q. Overall, do you consider advertising a good or bad thing?			
Very bad	0	0	1
Somewhat bad	2	0	1
Neither bad nor good	13	48	7
Somewhat good	36	50	32
Very good	6	8	2
Q. Overall, do you like or dislike advertising?			
Strongly dislike it	0	3	1
Somewhat dislike it	2	2	11
Feel neutral	13	48	27
Somewhat like it	32	48	3
Strongly like it	10	5	1

TABLE 3. Perceptions of the Uses and Consequences of Advertising[†]

	All three n = 205	Singapore n = 56 (a)	Malaysia n = 106 (b)	Hong Kong n = 43 (c)
Marketplace Information				
• Adv. is a valuable source of information about local sales.	4.95	4.91	5.05	4.69
• Adv. tells me which brands have the features I am looking for.	4.77	4.82	4.87	4.45
• Adv. keeps me up-to-date about products available in the market.	5.61	5.81	5.56	5.62
Buying Confidence				
• One can put more trust in products that are advertised than in those that are not.	3.84	3.84	3.81	3.98
• Adv. helps the consumer buy the best brand for the price.	3.48*	3.65	3.58	3.00_a
• If there were no adv., deciding what to buy would be difficult.	4.41	4.49	4.49	4.21
Social-Image Information				
• Adv. tells me what people like myself are buying and using.	4.13	4.37	4.04	4.36
• Adv. helps me know which products will or will not help me reflect the sort of person I am.	4.04	4.47	3.90	4.24
• From adv. I learn what is in fashion and what I should buy for keeping a good social image.	4.69	4.96	4.48	5.07
Entertainment Value				
• Sometimes I take pleasure in thinking about what I heard or saw in advertising.	4.83	4.82	4.75	5.10
• Some advertising makes me feel good.	4.93*	4.74	4.75	5.52_{ab}
• Sometimes TV commercials are even more enjoyable than TV programs.	4.44*	4.25	4.10	5.38_{ab}
Materialism				
• Adv. is making us into a materialistic society interested in buying and owning things.	5.15	5.05	5.16	4.90
• Adv. makes people buy unaffordable products just to show off.	4.48*	4.91	4.58	4.07_a
• Adv. sometimes makes people live in a world of fantasy.	4.86	5.23	4.69	5.10

TABLE 3 (continued)

	All three $n = 205$	Singapore $n = 56$ (a)	Malaysia $n = 106$ (b)	Hong Kong $n = 43$ (c)
Value Congruence				
• In adv. I often see my own values and beliefs portrayed.	4.01	4.09	3.93	4.05
• A lot of adv. is based on ideas and values which are opposite to my own.	4.20	4.16	4.05	4.57
• There is too much sex in advertising.	3.17**	3.33	2.78$_{ac}$	4.02
Effects on Children				
• Adv. leads children to make unreasonable purchase demands on parents.	5.58	5.67	5.58	5.40
• Adv. takes advantage of children.	5.06	5.23	5.15	4.79
• Adv. plays an important role in educating children about what products are good for them.	3.29	3.61	3.21	3.26
Economic Effects				
• Adv. improves people's standard of living.	4.40	4.60	4.29	4.29
• Adv. increases the costs of products.	5.85	5.88	5.77	5.93
• It would be best for companies to save money on adv. and invest the money on improving the product.	4.67	4.93	4.75	4.57
• If adv. were eliminated consumers would be better off.	3.55	3.39	3.57	3.48
Free TV				
• We need TV commercials to support TV programming.	4.75	4.75	4.58$_c$	5.26
Manipulation				
• Adv. makes you buy what you do not need.	4.48	4.86	4.49	4.43
• Sometimes I have bought things simply because of a TV commercial.	4.17	4.42	4.09	4.26
• I am never really persuaded by adv. to buy a product.	3.62	3.40	3.70	3.57
Cronbach alpha	.8167	.7823	.8310	.8161

[†] Along a scale of 1 (low) to 7 (high)
** Results of ANOVA significant at $p < .01$.
* Results of ANOVA significant at $p < .05$.
a/b/c subscript represents significantly different country means for each variable at $p < .05$. by pairwise comparison.

high (mean = 3.84), most conceded that in the absence of advertising, decision-making would in fact be more difficult (mean = 4.41). In terms of social image information, it would appear as if advertising does act as a fairly good social barometer, keeping consumers in touch with the marketplace. Furthermore, most respondents acknowledged that (TV) advertising still holds entertainment value–another optimistic finding for Asian marketers.

With regard to some of the less desirable consequences of advertising, most respondents agreed that advertising is making society more materialistic (mean = 5.15). However, in terms of value congruence, a surprisingly high proportion of respondents could in fact relate to the values portrayed in advertising (possibly slightly exaggerated due to a more controlled advertising industry in many Asian countries). By contrast, most respondents held fairly strong beliefs regarding the (negative) effects of advertising on children. This could, to some degree, be due to the more conservative approach to child-rearing common in many Asian countries (Naisbitt, 1995). Respondents by and large echoed the fairly common economic criticisms of advertising, but as with buying confidence, they did acknowledge that advertising is at worst a necessary evil–in that consumers would not be better off in the absence of advertising. Lastly, on the fairly subjective and somewhat controversial issue of manipulation, a number of respondents admitted being persuaded by advertising–to the point of perhaps even making unjustified purchases.

At 0.78, 0.83 and 0.82, coefficient alphas for the questionnaire are greater than the 0.7 suggested by Nunnally (1978), and can therefore be deemed acceptable.

In comparing the three populations, a number of interesting statistically significant differences were observed: particularly for Hong Kong Xers, who have the least confidence in advertising (mean = 3.0), are considerably more appreciative of entertaining advertising (mean = 5.52) and are less convinced that advertising contributes to materialism (mean = 4.07) than their Asian neighbors. Malaysian Xers, not surprisingly, do not feel that there is too much sex in advertising (mean = 2.78)–given that country's fairly strictly regulated and censored industry.

DISCUSSION

Young Asians appear to have a more positive attitude towards advertising than their American counterparts (or at least the popular stereotype of young Americans). Asian Xers are eager recipients of advertising despite the fact that in terms of value congruence they tend not to see their own values being portrayed in most ads, view advertising as making them more materialistic, and leads children to make unreasonable demands on parents. However, they tend to feel that if advertising is eliminated, consumers would not be better off. Advertising seems to provide assistance in deciding what to buy when it is difficult and keeps them informed and up to date especially about what is in fashion and what should be bought for keeping a good social image. The message seems to be: we know that in some respects it is not good for us, but isn't it great! The issue of advertising providing the audience with the ability to keep a good social image appears to be a particularly important aspect in many Asian countries.

In the light of these findings, it seems that regional marketers can confidently be more aggressive (less apologetic) in their efforts to communicate with the segment. Given the tremendous potential of the region generally, and the cohort specifically, this is perhaps the single most substantive finding of the study. If anything, the managerial implications for Asian marketers, as well as (American) MNCs competing in the region, would be to ignore popular (unverified) stereotypes, while at the same time not becoming complacent and concentrating rather on simultaneously developing other media strategies, while continuing to maintain a strong above-the-line presence.

CONCLUSIONS

Perhaps Douglas Coupland's novel, a tale of languid youths musing over "mental ground zero–the location where one visualizes oneself during the dropping of the atomic bomb: frequently a shopping mall" (Hornblower, 1997), was not written with young Asians in mind. In fact, it could be that the popular media and marketing press may have read a little too deeply between the lines. If, as Mittal (1994) suggests, the health of advertising can be defined by the public acceptance of it, our study shows the patient to be fit and well, and certainly not suspected of displaying signs of hypochondria. Half of Asian Xers actually like advertising, and nearly two thirds consider it to be a 'good thing.' The overwhelming majority deem the institution to be both essential, and more specifically, important to them personally. In summary, they are paying attention, and are positively disposed. These findings do not give the industry any reason to become complacent. On the contrary, Xers are something of a moving target, and are certainly more informed, and more rational consumers than their parents. They object to puffery and gratuitous sexual appeals, and are looking for added value at a reasonable price. Marketers in the region would do well to augment their above the line efforts with other media. Direct marketing, for example, can contribute to the two things Barrow (1994) maintains Generation X needs most–*outstanding value* and a *personal relationship*. In addition, it is important to remember that the cohort is exceptionally adept and comfortable with technology both as a marketing medium and for personal consumption. They literally 'grew up' using computers and are therefore more likely to use on-line services to make retail purchases than any other group (Litvan, 1996). The next decade in particular will indeed be an exciting time for marketers and consumers in Asia.

LIMITATIONS AND DIRECTIONS FOR FUTURE RESEARCH

First, the 29 items together measure attitudes regarding the consequences of advertising. In terms of the questionnaire's psychometric properties, reliability was confirmed, but validity still needs to be rigorously tested. Such tests would require the determination of measurement equivalence across the different cultures considered. A second limitation concerns the size of the samples in the different countries, which may not be sufficiently representative. Finally, gender representation in all three samples is biased towards females, and in the case of the Malaysian sample, is rather skewed towards the younger respondents within the cohort.

Future research might focus on more cross-cultural comparisons with larger samples that would allow further testing for reliability and validity of the questionnaire. Future research should not neglect the fact that reported quality standards of a scale in terms of reliability and validity may be influenced by cultural factors and that any inequivalence can severely diminish the usefulness of findings. The effect of (Xers') attitudes to advertising on their intentions to purchase is a rich area for research that is of considerable practical importance to firms operating in the region, as well as those firms looking to introduce brands that have been successful in other parts of the world. In addition, it would be interesting to see to what degree our findings in developing/recently developed countries are mirrored in more mature markets (like the US, Australia or England). Lastly, future research might investigate Asian Xers' 'role models,' from the point of using celebrity endorsers in advertising (do the 'antiheros' like Kurt Cobain and Dennis Rodman have a place in Asia?).

REFERENCES

Aaker, D.A. and Bruzzone, D.E. (1981). Viewer Perceptions of Prime-Time Television Advertising, *Journal of Advertising Research*, 21, 5, 15-23.

Adams, M. (1996). Larry Flynt is all the 'Rage,' *Mediaweek*, (March), 6(12), 23.

Appelbaum, C. (1992). As Cola Sales Dip, Pepsi Turns on Mountain Dew, *Adweek's Marketing Week*, (February) p. 6.

Ariga, M., Yasue, M. and Gu, X.W. (1997). China's Generation III. Viable target segment and implications for marketing communications, *Marketing and Research Today*, 25, 1, 17-24.

Barrow, P. (1994). Marketing to Generation X, *Canadian Manager*, (March), 19, 1, 23-24.

Biel, A.L. and Bridgwater, C.A. (1990). Attributes of Likable Television Commercials, *Journal of Advertising Research*, 30, 3, 39-43.

Brunelli, R. (1994). Neon lights the Motor City, *Brandweek*, (June), 35(26), S2-S3.

Chang, H. (1996). In Singapore the dreams are getting bigger, *Business Week*, Sep 23, 20-21.

DeCoursey, J. (1996). Claiborne throws a curve at young men and women, *Advertising Age*, (April), 67(16), 20.

Donaton, S. (January 1). The Media Wakes Up To Generation X, *Advertising Age*, pp. 16-17.

Ewing, M.T. and Pascual, A. (1997) *A Geodemographic Exploration for Generation X^{ASIA}: Marketing Myth or Psychographic Reality?* Unpublished Working Paper, School of Marketing, Curtin University of Technology, Perth, Western Australia.

Freeman, L. (1995a). Advertising's mirror is cracked, *Advertising Age*, (February), 66(6), 30.

Freeman, L. (1995b). No tricking the media savvy, *Advertising Age*, (February), 66(6), 30.

Freeman, L. (1996). Trendy sport-utility fords across generation gap, *Advertising Age*, (April), 67(14), S24.

Giles, J. (1994, June 6). Generalizations X, *Newsweek*, pp. 62-67.

Gossage, H.L. (1986). Is Advertising Worth Saving? In *Is There Any Hope for Advertising?* Howard Luck Gossage et al., eds. Urbana: University of Illinois Press.

Gustafson, R. (1994). Marketing to Generation X? Better practice safe sex, *Advertising Age*, (March), 65(10), 26.

Harrington, S. (1995). 'In between young, foolish & old, boring', *Advertising Age*, (February), 66(6), 28.

Hornblower, M. (1997). Great Expectations, *Time*, June 9, 54-60.

Horton, C. and Serafin, R. (1993). X Marks the Spot for Car Marketing, *Advertising Age* (Aug), 8.

Huhn, M. (1994). Meaning a thing by launching 'Swing,' *Adweek*, (April), 35(15), 10.

Isler, E. (1994). Twenty-somethings talk to themselves, *Folio: The Magazine for Magazine Management [FOL]*, (May), 23(8), 21.

Jensen, T. (1996). Needham aims Budweiser toward younger crowd in 'K.O.B.' campaign, *Adweek* (May), 37(21), 5.

Jensen, J. (1994). Comics' high-tech weapons, *Advertising Age*, (September), 65(38), 20, 24.

Johnson, J. (1996). Generation X: Problems ahead, *Discount Merchandiser*, (February), 36(2), 18.

Kjellberg, N. (1994). Coors Light cans offer a sunny surprise, *Brandweek*, (July), 35(29), 18.

Kirkpatrick, J. (1986). A Philosophic Defense of Advertising, *Journal of Advertising Research*, 15, 2, 28-42.

Leo, J. (October). Madison Avenue's Gender War, *U.S. News & World Report*, p. 25.

Light, L. (1990). The Changing Advertising World, *Journal of Advertising Research*, Feb/Mar, 30-35.

Litvan, L. (1996). X marks the spot for low key sales, *Nation's Business*, U. S. Chamber of Commerce (http://www.speakeasy.org/press/natbus.html).

Macalister, K. (1994). The X generation, *HR Magazine*, (May), 39(5), 66-71.

Marchetti, M. (1995). Free advice from a 'slacker,' *Sales & Marketing Management [SAL]*, (December), 147(12), 68.

McCarthy, M. and Parpis, E. (1995). Open the top, let down your hair, *Adweek*, (September), 16(37), 37.

Mittal, B. (1994). Public Assessment of TV Advertising: Faint Praise and Harsh Criticism, *Journal of Advertising Research*, (January/February), 35-53.

Naisbitt, J. (1995). *Megatrends Asia*, Nicholas Brealey Publishing: London.

Nunnally, J. C. (1978). *Psychometric Theory*, New York: McGraw-Hill, 2ed.

Ogilvy, D. (1983). *Ogilvy on Advertising*, New York: Crown Publishers.

Pollay, R.W. and Mittal, B. (1993). Here's the Beef: Factors, Determinants, and Segments in Consumer Criticisms of Advertising, *Journal of Marketing* 57, 3, 99-114.

Rubel, C. (1996). Soft drink makers place future in youths' hands, *Marketing News*, (May), 30(11), 18.

Schlinger, M. J. (1979). A Profile of Responses to Commercials, *Journal of Advertising Research*, 19, 2, 37-46.

Shimp, T. (1997). *Advertising, Promotion, and Supplemental Aspects of Integrated Marketing Communications*, Orlando FL: The Dryden Press.

Stipp, H. (1994). Xers are not created equal, *Mediaweek*, (March), 4(12), 20.

Verzone, R. (1996). Younger consumers want education, accessibility, *Best's Review*, (February), 96(10), 74.

West, D. (1995). Insurers are starting to pick up on 'Generation X,' *National Underwriter*, (October), 99(43), 7, 29.

Segmenting China's Consumer Market: A Hybrid Approach

Geng Cui

SUMMARY. China as one of the Big Emerging Markets (BEMs) has attracted increasing trade and foreign investment in the past two decades. The emergence of China as a viable consumer market has created tremendous opportunities for multinational corporations (MNCs). Meanwhile, continuous evolution of the economy and increasing heterogeneity of Chinese consumers challenge foreign marketers to accurately assess market demand and to enact effective marketing strategies. This research proposes to segment China's consumer market using a hybrid approach including demographics, psychographics and geographics. It also examines several other notable characteristics of the Chinese consumer market and draws marketing strategy implications for MNCs. *[Article copies available for a fee from The Haworth Document Delivery Service: 1-800-342-9678. E-mail address: getinfo@haworthpressinc.com]*

KEYWORDS. China's consumer market, segmentation, marketing strategy

Too often, China seems to have existed to a large extent in the eyes of foreign beholders, . . . As in most countries, the situation in China has rarely been all black or all white; almost always it has been some shade of gray.

–A. Doak Barnett (1993)

Geng Cui is affiliated with the Department of Marketing, School of Business, Howard University, Washington, DC 20059 USA (E-mail: gcui@fac.howard.edu).

[Haworth co-indexing entry note]: "Segmenting China's Consumer Market: A Hybrid Approach." Cui, Geng. Co-published simultaneously in *Journal of International Consumer Marketing* (International Business Press, an imprint of The Haworth Press, Inc.) Vol. 11, No. 1, 1999, pp. 55-76; and: *Consumer Behavior in Asia: Issues and Marketing Practice* (ed: T. S. Chan) International Business Press, an imprint of The Haworth Press, Inc., 1999, pp. 55-76. Single or multiple copies of this article are available for a fee from The Haworth Document Delivery Service [1-800-342-9678, 9:00 a.m. - 5:00 p.m. (EST). E-mail address: getinfo@haworthpress inc.com].

55

INTRODUCTION

In the past two decades, China has experienced rapid economic growth and become one of the biggest Big Emerging Markets (BEMs). The rise of China as a viable consumer market has important economic implications for western nations. China alone, for instance, constitutes the US' third largest export market and has the second largest trade surplus against the US. From now until well into the 21st century, realization of China's market potential will be a major stimulus to economic growth in East Asia and the rest of the world. China's economic growth in the years to come will continue to create a plethora of opportunities as well as daunting challenges for multinational corporations (MNCs). As more MNCs continue to converge in this market, understanding China's consumers, its market structure and implications for marketing strategies is essential for successful China operations. Two common problems that MNCs face in China are accurate assessment of consumer demand for their products and effective marketing strategies. This research proposes to segment the Chinese consumer market using a hybrid approach including demographics, psychographics and geographics, and draws marketing strategy implications for MNCs.

THE LAND OF OPPORTUNITIES

An overview of China's economy highlights the attractiveness of the growing market. The geographic area of China is slightly bigger than that of the United States. China's population is 1.25 billion, thus roughly every one of four human beings on earth is a native speaker of the Chinese language. Although China's population density is relatively low compared to some other countries, most Chinese reside along the coastline, making it a highly concentrated market. The country's birth rate is much higher than those of Western nations, resulting in a younger population. At the macro-economic level, its GDP reached $650 billion in 1996. With an import of about $100 billion per year, China represents an enormous market, rivaling that of a European economy. Its potential purchasing power, measured by the international reserves, came to a total of $65 billion in 1996. In the last two decades, Chinese government has opened one industry after another for foreign participation. As part of the campaign to joint the World Trade Organization (WTO), China has reduced tariffs and the number of products requiring import licenses, revised customs laws, and strengthened intellectual property protection.

Economic expansion of China has attracted increasing trade and foreign investment. Using the Purchase Power Parity (PPP) method, the International

Monetary Fund in 1992 already ranked China as the world's third largest economy with a $1.7 trillion GNP in local currency's purchasing power (Nomani 1993). If China's economy continues to grow at the rate of 10% per annum, its GNP could reach $2.8 trillion by 2005 (Hamlin 1994). The rapid economic expansion was initially driven by the transfer of labor-intensive operations from Hong Kong, Taiwan and other countries to the mainland. In more recent years, MNCs flocked to China, selling products from passenger jets to baby food, to serve the pent-up consumer demand. Major MNCs have taken positions in China, attempting to block out slower-moving competitors. Success stories such as Coca-Cola and Avon's tremendous growth entice more entrants to the market. The attraction of business opportunities in China is epitomized by the encouraging words one would say today to an ambitious merchant "Go West, young man–to the East!"

Given its enormous size and presumably homogeneous culture, China promises many opportunities for growth and expansion, and for improving efficiency using standardized marketing. China has over 70 major newspapers and magazines, about twenty of which have a circulation over one million. The number of radio receivers is over 200 million (Europa World Yearbook 1995). With 36 million sets, television has become a popular advertising vehicle. Several large networks such as CCTV can cover the entire country. The Chinese written language is the same for the Han Chinese, 94% of the population, with some regional variations in dialects. Thus, standardized advertising in the Chinese language is plausible for the whole market. Such an appearance of a homogeneous market has led many to dream of reaching the 1.2 billion consumers–"If every Chinese buys one of our products, . . ."

In the face of major political, social and economic changes sweeping China, some MNCs believe that the often-elusive market is finally becoming lucrative. Since 1992, China has welcomed broad-based foreign participation in the retail sector. Foreign-funded manufacturing companies are permitted to sell their output in the domestic market as long as they balance their foreign exchange. Rapid increases in consumer income and changing spending patterns have driven up sales of many consumer goods. China's retail market, currently estimated at about $200 billion a year, is expected to grow at more than 20% per annum. For instance, sales of cosmetics grew from 9 billion RMB in 1994 to 18.2 billion RMB in 1996. Attracted by these rapidly multiplying figures, several MNCs, such as Yaohan of Japan, had ambitious plans to open hundreds of retail outlets in China.

The reality set in after the initial euphoria. Despite the publicity surrounding the new-found spending power of China's 1.2 billion people, foreign retailers soon discovered that the immense mainland population had not translated easily into a heady stream of customers. A significant number of

MNCs operating in China were not profitable (Rheem 1996). Many foreign ventures suffered from sluggish sales, escalating overhead costs, an inefficient local work force, and the omnipresent Chinese bureaucracy. Hasting to expand the scale of operation in the country without fully understanding the indigenous consumers has contributed to less than gratifying returns. Many MNCs have recognized that making inroads into China requires in-depth understanding of its consumers, long-term planning, and differentiated marketing (Cui 1997). A summary of their experiences suggests two major concerns that MNCs have about marketing in China: accurate assessment of consumer demand and effective marketing strategies.

The popular press has written much about China's economic potential. Yet until recently, there has been no systematic analysis of its consumers and marketing implications. Most research has focused on the economic, political and market barriers to access the Chinese market. They failed to address the fundamental marketing issues such as the market size for various products and effective marketing mix strategies. A major cause of this confusion is the often too optimistic misconception that China has a largely homogeneous group of consumers with increasing disposable income, crazing for imported goods. Although there appears to be some truth to this depiction in the eyes of a foreign beholder, any attempt to approach China with this monolithic view of the market is at best inadequate.

IN SEARCH OF THE CHINESE CONSUMER

An important indicator of attractive market opportunities, now present in a number of Asian economies, is a growing and affluent middle class looking for quality products. Despite the optimism about China, MNCs often have difficulty in accurately estimating the effective purchasing power of Chinese consumers. Official statistics indicate the per capita income in China was $681 in 1996. Many believe this figure undercounts the real earnings and buying power of Chinese consumers, especially in the cities where non-wage income and subsidies count as much as one-third of a person's total income (Zhao 1993). The International Monetary Fund, using the PPP method, estimated the average Chinese consumer's annual purchasing power ranged between $1,950 and $2,598, a level at which substantial consumption should become apparent (Piturro 1994). If this trend continues, China's average personal income could reach $11,000 by 2010. With no mortgage obligation, largely free medical care and public education, low rents, no income tax except for a few, they are able to save up to 40% of their income. These consumers are, if not richer as individuals, in aggregate bigger than those in Japan. Thus, China is still the largest untapped consumer market in the world.

Several studies have surveyed the Chinese consumers to size up their purchasing power. In a study of 280 well-off people in Shanghai and Guangzhou, Roper Research International found that these "super consumers" earned 10 times the average annual income in China, and 85% of them preferred to purchase items with cash (Gavin 1994). Many of these super consumers are entrepreneurs, professionals in private companies, and workers in township enterprises. However, the average Chinese hardly fits the profile of a "super consumer." In reality, the typical Chinese consumer is mostly likely in the twenties, with limited income, living in an apartment with their parents. In mid-1994, Gallup China Ltd. conducted the first national consumer survey by a foreign research company in China (Li and Gallup 1995). Based on a sample of 3,400 people representing the entire adult population in China, Gallup uncovered a consumer who is generally pragmatic and plans carefully for purchases. While Western goods are often better quality and important for social status, and Chinese consumers clearly prefer imported quality products, they are far more sophisticated and discriminating than anticipated (Cui 1997). Most Chinese are rather value conscious and would not simply buy anything.

Despite its well publicized 1.2 billion consumers, China is largely a developing country and hardly represents a single market. Focusing on the rising income alone as the indication of market attractiveness creates an inaccurate perception of the opportunities and risks there. Regional differences in the level of economic development, infrastructure, consumer purchasing power, distribution and transportation logistics, can erect major stumbling blocks for MNCs to exercise a standardized approach to the market. In addition, the Chinese have diverse cultural patterns exhibited by variations in dialects, taste, temperament and lifestyles (Xu 1990). As many products have reached the growth and maturity stage of the product life cycle, and as MNCs move beyond the peripheral coastal cities and expand into inland regions, they need to consider discrepant consumer purchasing power and lifestyles as well as regional differences to accurately assess market demand and to enact effective marketing strategies.

A Hybrid Approach to Market Segmentation

Market segmentation is critical for understanding the structure of a market, exploring the divergent needs of heterogeneous consumer groups, and identifying entry and expansion opportunities. Demographic and psychographic characteristics of consumers such as income, education and personality together shape their consumption behavior and marketing responses (Engel, Fiorillo and Cayley 1972; Plummer 1974). Over the years, market segmentation based on consumer demographics and psychographics has become an antecedent to effective marketing strategies. In China where the market has become more fragmented, market segmentation and targeted marketing have become increasingly important for successful marketing operations. The profile of a single group or the "average" Chinese consumer hardly depicts the diversity in consumption patterns among the Chinese. In reality, China consists of multiple markets segmented by income, age, consumer values and lifestyles, regional economic development, and local culture. Thus, a hybrid approach to segmenting China's consumer market using multiple dimensions is well advised.

Although substantial commonalties exist among the Chinese, foreign companies will not find a majority middle class like that in Japan or the US. On the contrary, China's market can be stratified on several key demographic and psychographic variables. Because imported goods and those made by foreign joint ventures are usually often more expensive than domestic products, income has a tremendous impact on purchase of foreign goods. So are education and occupation, which significantly correlated with consumer purchasing power. Psychographic factors such as innovativeness and risk aversion also affect consumer readiness for purchasing foreign goods. Consumers' orientation towards the future and lifestyles are also important predictors of their willingness to buy (Plummer 1974; Wei 1997).

Location of residence is another important factor. There are significant differences in income and attitudes between people in rural and urban areas. While those who work in China's booming coastal cities now have a substantial disposable income, 70% of China's 1.2 billion people are peasants and still largely live hand-to-mouth. Urban dwellers make up about 30% of the national population yet account for 50% of their total income. For instance, urban residents in China's top 16 cities–16.9% of the national population, account for 33% of the national retail sales. The retail market boom, growing at an average 30% per annum, is basically an urban phenomenon (Lim 1996). Furthermore, regional disparity in economic development also plays a key role in consumers' income and consumption patterns. The geoclusters for Western goods are essentially limited to the south and eastern parts of China's urban areas and the people with high disposable income. Thus, the bases for segmenting China's consumer market should include all three dimensions: demographics, psychographics, and geographics.

Considering the above dimensions, China's consumers can be grouped into four segments (Table 1). Atop the list, the "Nouveau Riche" (*baofahu*) class is the most attractive. Some estimate there are 100,000 to 200,000 such people in China, and the number is steadily growing. They essentially include entrepreneurs, business people, celebrities, and government officials of various ranks, who have benefited the most from the opportunities created by the reforms and privatization. They concentrate in China's booming coastal cities and other major metropolitan areas. These are the super spenders who gross over $5,000 a year, much higher than the average Chinese household. They

TABLE 1. A Hybrid Approach to Segmenting Chinese Consumers

Segment/ Attribute	Nouveau Riche (baofahu)	Yuppies (dushi yapishi)	Salary Class (gongxin jieceng)	Working Poor (qionglaogong)
Size of Segment	100,000	60 million	300 million	840 million
Geographics Residence Place	coastal urban areas	major urban areas	small cities	small towns and rural areas
Demographics Household Income Age Education Occupation	above $5,000 30-65 various entrepreneurs business people govn't officials celebrities	$2,000-$5,000 25-45 college managerial professional technical	$1,000-$1,999 18-60 high school office clerks factory workers teachers	less than $1,000 all age groups elementary school manual laborers peasants migrant workers
Psychographics Orientation Innovativeness Risk Aversion Readiness for foreign goods	optimistic innovators trend-setters low high	hopeful early adopters opinion leaders moderate moderate	status quo early majority emulators high low	uncertain late majority and laggards very high minimum
Lifestyles Mobility Activities	active wheel & deal, dine & wine in exclusive clubs frequent shopping binges	mobile busy work schedule, freq- quent dining out & excursions	confined trapped 8 to 5, limited disposable income, occa- sional outings, cameras and parks	immobile menial labor, hand-to-mouth, "mass" style entertainment such as sports on TV

Notes:
1. The houshold income figures in this table are based on reports from various organizations such as the International Monetary Fund, World Bank and the Gallup Organization.
2. The terms in parentheses such as *baofahu* and *dushi yapishi* are the romanized Chinese (pin yin) idioms for the respective market segments.

may possess a cellular phone, a private automobile, a credit card, and even a luxury dwelling. These consumers maintain a very active lifestyle, dining and wining in exclusive clubs. They have traveled overseas and may spend their vacations in Southeast Asia. In general, they are very optimistic about the future. With newfound wealth and undaunted by the hefty prices, their aversion to risk is minimal. Being the innovators among the Chinese, they are eager to acquire imported prestige products and show off their status.

The Yuppies' (*dushi yapishi*) group is composed of people in the ages between 25-45, with at least some college education or technical training, residing in major metropolitan areas (Table 1). These Chinese, approximately 60 million of them, work in China's new enterprises, joint ventures and foreign companies. They are professionals in managerial and technical positions, and small business owners, thus receiving handsome compensations by Chinese standards. Their household income ranges from $2,000 to $5,000 per annum. These younger and better-educated consumers have separated themselves from the traditions of the past, and in many cases from the government as their employer. They are experimenting with new lifestyles and are more responsive to new ideas and products from the West. Full of hope for the future, they work hard and have ambitious plans to enhance their quality of life. They have begun to develop some discriminating tastes and become the early adopters among the Chinese consumers. Many of them place premium value on quality and convenience, shop at modern grocery stores, and make occasional excursions. This group, together with the "Nouveau Riche," are the prime consumers of foreign products. Thus, the real size of the consumer market that can afford foreign goods is approximately 5% of the population, scattered around the country in pockets of wealthy cities (Murray 1994). These consumers in prosperous coastal cities and major urbanites are the emerging middle-class consumers in China.

The Salary Class (*gongxin jieceng*) are essentially workers who are still trapped in jobs with the state enterprises for a fixed salary and some bonus, and those township enterprise workers who are making a decent living (Table 1). They faithfully commute to their "work units" and perform the daily routines. Providing their work units are profitable, they may get paid on time and have their medical expenses covered. Their annual household income ranges from $1,000 to $1,999. They most closely resemble the average Chinese consumer, which accounts for 25% of the population. With an escalating inflation of more than 10% per year, their disposable income has not grown that much. Thus, they are more concerned with maintaining the status quo. As followers and emulators, they hold positive attitudes towards foreign goods. But with meager incomes, they can afford foreign products only by spending their long-term savings to purchase major appliances. In most cases, they "wait and see" before deciding on a major acquisition, and put greater emphasis on value. Thus, their purchase of imported goods tends to be infrequent, delayed and deliberate. With minimal mobility, they are confined to occasional outings to the parks with cameras. They essentially belong to the early majority group in purchasing new products.

The vast majority of Chinese, approximately 70% of the population, belongs to the group of "Working Poor" (*qionglaogong*). The least educated, with no marketable skills, and the most disadvantaged in reaping the benefits of reforms, most of them engage in manual labor in small state and township enterprises. They also include the millions of displaced workers, retirees on a fixed pension, and the majority of China's peasants. Their household income falls below $1,000. Rural households make even less, and the urban-rural gap seems to be widening (Clayton 1995). Many of their work units are unprofitable state enterprises. Imported foreign goods, often of better quality, are beyond their reach. Conservative and need-driven, they fear being left out and are uncertain about the prospect of the future, and may be nostalgic about the old days when things were more predictable. Thus, they are less innovative and highly aversive to risks. With limited means, they more often opt to buy domestic products and local brands that are less expensive. They are immobile and favor "mass" style entertainment such as sports on TV. However, many peasants who live near major metropolitan areas are better off than those city workers on a fixed salary. But they are not typical of the average live-off-the-land Chinese peasant.

Although the rising income of an emerging middle class has been the indicator of market opportunities in some Asian countries, China is far less homogeneous. The above segments largely represent four distinct groups of Chinese consumers, each with its own unique profile of demographic, psychographic, and geographic characteristics. Although all four consumer segments are identifiable and measurable, only the Nouveau Riche and the Yuppies are truly accessible, responsive and susceptible to the appeals of foreign products. They are the prime consumers of imported goods, particularly luxury items. Depending on the product category and the stage of product life cycle, evaluation of the attractiveness of each segment should be the starting point for identifying market opportunities, assessing demand, forecasting sales, and deriving marketing strategies.

China's Eight Regional Markets

For MNCs seeking entry and expansion in China, it is important to recognize that China actually is a conglomeration of fragmented markets divided by factors such as level of economic development, industrial priorities and local cultures. Like many large states, China is a multi-ethnic country with heterogeneous subcultures. Behind the Great Wall, there are 50 ethnic groups. Even among the Han nationality, there is tremendous diversity in speech, culture and tradition. Furthermore, regional environmental conditions such as topography and climate also have a tremendous impact on economic development and help in shaping consumer attitudes and lifestyles (Sum 1997). Each region, for instance, has its own distinctive culinary traditions, music and operatic styles. Studies in North America suggest that regional differences in economy, culture and consumer attitudes result in distinctive markets, which require differentiated marketing strategies (Garreau 1981). Likewise, based on economic development, local culture and consumer attitudes, China can be divided into eight distinctive regional markets (Figure 1). These regional markets can be grouped into three levels of market

FIGURE 1. China's Eight Regional Markets

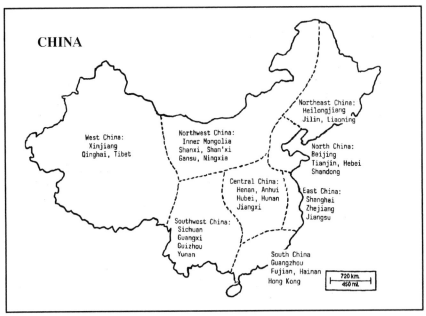

Note: The regional boundaries are simplified and do not reflect the actual demarcations.

development and consumer readiness: growth markets, emerging markets, and untapped markets (Table 2).

First, government policy to "let some people get rich first" created tremendous economic disparity between coastal cities and hinterland regions (Khan, Griffin, Risk and Zhao 1993). The eastern part of the country has the top three growth markets: South China, East China and North China. Following the "open door" policy, China's coastal areas were the first to attract outside investment and have benefited the most from economic reforms (Yeung and Hu 1992). All four Special Economic Zones (SEZs) and fourteen "Open Cities" are located on China's coast line, providing generous provisions for corporate tax, import and export duties, and other privileges. They are the most advanced in economic infrastructure and market development. All these regions tend to have higher per capita income than other areas. For instance, the top five markets including Guangdong, Jiangsu, Zhejiang, Shanghai and Beijing have 16.9% of the country's population yet accounted for 33% of national retail sales (Lim 1996).

South China includes Guangdong, Hainan, and Fujian Provinces (Table 2).

TABLE 2. China's Eight Regional Markets

Regional Market	Cities & Provinces	Market Characteristics	Economy, Culture and Quality of Life
South China (huanan)	Guangdong, Fujian, Hainan and Hong Kong	"Growth markets" in coastal areas with open cities and metropolitan areas, attract the most foreign investment and account for much of the economic activity. Its consumers are wealthy and educated trendsetters.	Outward-oriented, fast growing and freewheeling, the regional economy is transforming from labor intensive operations to high tech manufacturing. Cantonese and Fukienese are the main dialects. Close to Hong Kong and Taiwan, its wealthy consumers emphasize materialism and conspicuous consumption.
East China (huadong)	Shanghai, Jiangsu and Zhejiang		The industrial powerhouse and financial center of the country, Shanghai leads the region in both industrial and agricultural output. Shanghainese is the main dialect. People have tremendous pride in local products and amenities. Consumers are cosmopolitan and innovative, setting trends in fashion and lifestyles.
North China (huabei)	Beijing, Tianjin, Hebei and Shandong		The geo-political center of the nation, Beijing leads the region in attracting foreign investment and growth in large state enterprises and strategic industries such as information technology. Representing the traditional Chinese culture, consumers are relatively conservative, emphasize intrinsic satisfaction yet open to new product ideas.
Northeast China (dongbei)	Liaoning, Jilin and Heilongjiang	"Emerging markets" in landlocked areas, with sound economic base, a huge population, and diverse cultures, they are positioned for growth, and attracting investment.	The "foundry" of the nation emphasizes its heavy industries in mining, automobile and machinery. Long winters produce limited agricultural output and variety. Consumers are conservative and less susceptible to outside influences.
Central China (zhongyuan)	Henan, Hubei, Hunan, Jiangxi and Anhui		With great emphasis on agriculture, the plains with depleted resources face perennial flood problems. Its economy has been repositioned for growth, building transportation hubs for the country. From diverse local cultures, consumers are trend followers.
Southwest China (xinan)	Sichuan, Yunan, Guizhou and Guangxi		The closed-in region is less accessible. With an enormous population and rich natural resources, it has great protential. The less spoiled environment attracts influx of tourists. Many ethnic minorities make it the most culturally diverse.
Northwest China (xibei)	Inner Mongolia, Shanxi, Shan'xi, Ningxia and Gansu	"Untapped markets" in the hinterlands, sparsely populated, and economically impoverished, are difficult to reach.	Led by the ancient capital of Xi'an, this region has, among the expanding desert, pastoral diary farms but a slow-moving economy. For the rugged hardship post, government is trying to reverse the trend by encouraging more investment in the region. Mongolians and Muslims are the ethnic minorities.
West China (xibu)	Xinjiang, Qinghai and Tibet		The "empty quarter" is sparsely populated by Muslims and Tibetans. With little industry, this region is still relatively backward and poor, just beginning to move into the modern world. Little is happening as far as foreign goods are concerned.

This regional economy has been the most outward-oriented, and in more recent years, is transforming itself from labor-intensive operations to high tech manufacturing. The four original SEZs are located in this region: Shenzhen, Zhuhai, Shantou and Xiamen, and have attracted the most foreign investment. Increasingly freewheeling and independent, Guangdong has become more integrated with the economy of Hong Kong. Measured by GDP, Guangdong has already surpassed Shanghai as the most productive region of the country. Fujian has attracted many investors across the strait from Taiwan, and is renewing its historical ties with the island. This region also represents the Chinese culture of the South, i.e., Min-Yue Culture, with plenty of contact with the outside world and great emphasis on mercantile entrepreneurship. Each province has its own main dialect, Cantonese and Fukienese. Consumers in this area, about 7% of the Chinese population, are among the most prosperous in China, and considered the trendsetters. Many of them have relatives living overseas and have long been exposed to foreign products. Close to the popular cultures from Hong Kong and Taiwan, they are inclined to emphasize materialism and conspicuous consumption.

East China, centered around the mouth of the Yangtse River, consists of the city of Shanghai and Zhejiang and Jiangsu provinces (Table 2). Densely populated and highly urbanized, this region historically has been the most prosperous in China, productive in both agriculture and industries. In recent years, this region has become China's industrial powerhouse, boasting 30% of the country's industrial output for the last several years (Batson 1996). Its Open Cities include Lianyungang, Nantong, Ningbo, Wenzhou and Zhanjiang. This region is also sprawling with medium-size cities that specialize in textile and light industry manufacturing, such as Wuxi, Suzhou and Zhangjiagang. Shanghai, known as the "head of the dragon," is the industrial and financial nerve center of China and the gateway to eastern China's 200 million consumers and other neighboring provinces. Shanghai is also the regional cultural nucleus, representing the "Hai-pai" culture, well known for having the best amenities and products for enhancing the quality of life, and the tremendous pride in local products. Shanghainese is the main dialect of the region, with many other variations. Compared to other parts of China except for the South, consumers in this regional market are better off, the most innovative and cosmopolitan, setting trends in fashion and lifestyles.

North China, including Beijing, Tianjin, and the provinces of Hebei and Shandong, has been growing fast over the last few years and attracted investments from many countries such as Japan, Korea and the US, including large foreign investors such as Motorola and General Motors. Close to the center, with access to key government relationships and buying agencies, this region is making a tremendous investment in state-owned enterprises and in industries such as telecommunications, computer technology, and pharmaceuticals. With port cities like Tianjin, Yantai and Qingdao, this regional economy is increasingly open. Beijing as the geo-political center of the nation for centuries also represents the culture of North China–the Jing-pai culture–the traditional Chinese culture, attaching great value to hierarchy, stability and control (Ariga, Yasue and Wen 1997). Beijing dialect (putonghua) is promoted as the standard Chinese speech. Shandong Province, the hometown of Confucius and the biggest agricultural province in China, also has the best township enterprises in China. Compared to the consumers in the South and East, they appear to be relatively more conservative and place importance on intrinsic satisfaction, yet still open to new product ideas.

The emerging markets in Northeast, Central and Southwest China are becoming increasingly important and need to be cultivated (Table 2). *Northeast China*, with the three provinces of Heilongjiang, Jilin and Liaoning and the port city of Dalian, has begun to enjoy the benefits from the reforms. As the "foundry" of the country, this region emphasizes its heavy industries such as mining, automobile and machinery, etc., found in industrial cities such as Shenyang, Changchun and Harbin. This region is trying to revitalize its economy and build modern industries. In recent years, the border trade with Russia has been booming. This is the far north region of China, thus having the longest winter and limited agricultural output and variety in food products, except for its forestry products. Consumers are less susceptible to outside influences and have relatively lower levels of awareness of foreign brands. Manchurians and Koreans are the biggest ethnic minorities in the region, having great impact on the local culture.

Central China and Southwest China, despite their own industrial and agricultural bases, are relatively less developed and less accessible due to their landlocked locations. *Central China* (or Zhong-yuan), including the provinces of Henan, Hubei, Hunan, Jiangxi and Anhui, is the heartland of China with a heavy emphasis on agriculture. With depleted resources, perennial flood problems during the monsoon season, and drought during the summer, this region as the flood plain has some of the most impoverished places of the country. In recent years, this region has been trying to energize its economy and catch up with coastal areas. Headed by the industrial city of Wuhan, they have shown more respectable growth than in the past. This region is also building some of the major transportation hubs for rail transportation with the European-Asia corridor, thus it is becoming important for reaching other parts of China. Although most of its residents are Han Chinese, these consumers have unique cultures such as cuisine and operatic styles. They are conservative, conformist belongers. With an enormous population and a growing economy, this region has emerged as an excellent opportunity for growth and expansion.

Southwest China including Yunan, Guizhou, Guangxi and the most populous province of Sichuan (over 110 million people), has always been of particular interest to foreign consumer goods manufacturers (Table 2). Despite its industrial output and tremendous population, most firms find the consumer market there sluggish (Batson 1996). The topography of mountain, plateau and basin makes this region closed-in and less accessible. Headed by the city of Chongqing, this region is expanding its economic base to develop various industries. In a country where pollution has become a national issue, its environment is probably the least spoiled. The subtropical forest in the far south is as exotic as Shangri-La, thus attracting a huge influx of tourists every year. This region has great potential as it has a rich endowment of natural resources. Many of China's ethnic minorities reside in this region with close ties to several countries in southeast Asia, making it the most culturally diverse region of the country.

The untapped markets of Northwest and West China still await to be explored (O'Leary 1994). *Northwest China* includes the provinces of Shanxi, Shan'xi, Inner Mongolia, Gansu and Ningxia. Xi'an, the nation's ancient capital and a tourist hot spot, is the cultural capital of the region. Among the expanding desert, this region has been known for its pastoral farms and dairy products. However, cultivation over several thousand years makes this region less arable. Many people consider the far western part of the region the rugged frontier land and a hardship post. Mongolian and Muslims are the major ethnic minorities of the region and play an important role in the local culture. Many of them have adopted the irrigation and farming methods, and even the lifestyles of the Han Chinese. But recent government policies encourage more foreign investment in this region, and it is gradually catching up to the coastal areas.

Compared to the dynamic and rapidly developing eastern provinces along China's coast, the wide-open space of *West China* including Xinjiang, Qinghai and Tibet, is relatively backward and poor (Barnett 1993). Largely occupied by Muslim and Tibetan ethnic minorities, which has resisted assimilation into the Han Chinese culture, this "empty quarter" is sparsely populated and the least accessible. While the small number of Han Chinese in this region resides in urban areas, ethnic minorities have largely retained their ethnic culture and lifestyle. Many of them are still horseback nomads. Until recently, there has been little industry if any in this region. Little is happening in the impoverished west as far as foreign consumer goods are concerned, but they have just begun to enter the modern world. Even though it has a rich endowment of natural resources, this region is the least explored by foreign investors. The Chinese government has been trying to reverse this trend by investing more heavily in this region and encouraging inter-regional cooperation, to ensure this vast corner of the country is not to be forgotten in its rush towards modernity.

It is important for MNCs to understand the overall market potential of China as well as regional differences (Aguignier 1988). Each regional market has its unique geographic typography, economic base, and cultural heritage. Consumers in various regions are also known to differ in values, lifestyles, and the extent of contact with the outside world. These differences will in turn influence people's perception of imported goods and their purchase readiness. Beside the factor of geography, these regional markets are also the creations of Chinese government policy. Inter-regional disparity has grown rapidly in recent years. The regionalism and inter-provincial rivalry may create tremendous hidden barriers between these markets requiring that MNCs seek a national marketing and distribution strategy. Such a degree of complexity makes entry decision and distribution strategies more complex. The economic disparity between coastal areas and interior provinces is also a potential factor for social unrest. Acutely aware of the perils of regional disparities, the Chinese government has recently reduced the special privileges granted only to the coastal SEZs, launched a *"fupin"* (help the poor) campaign, and encouraged more investment in the hinterland areas. The gap between regions will be smaller as government tries to reverse the disparity and may clear away the barriers for regional cooperation.

Other Notable Market Characteristics

Other demographic dimensions such as gender and age can also result in meaningful and substantial market segments. For instance, the women's market exhibits unique characteristics and tremendous opportunities for household items, cosmetics and skin care products (Sum 1997). Products with convenience features will be very attractive to "working mothers," who strive to fulfill their professional and family roles. Age can also produce several significant markets. China's one-child-per-family has resulted in a generation of "Little Emperors and Empresses," who are pampered by both parents and four grandparents, creating tremendous market opportunities for products from food to educational aids (Johnstone 1996). The youth market–China's Generation III, also presents distinctive opportunities for creative marketing strategies (Ariga, Yasue and Wen 1997). The "mature" market is largely ignored by foreign marketers. However, retirees and older consumers present a significant market for various products such as personal medical aids and pharmaceuticals. In addition, sales of foreign products may also be subject to the impact of brand awareness and perception. Thus, the nature of a product category plays a key role in determining the proper dimensions for market segmentation.

Although regional disparities in economic development and consumer purchasing power have significant impact on consumption patterns, demand for many products may be subject to the impact of other factors. The size of different consumer segments is not proportional across various regions. Overall, the groups of Nouveau Riche and Yuppies are much larger in China's coastal areas. Residents in Shanghai, for instance, may earn three times as much as those urban residents in a mountain region like Guizhou. Meanwhile, the urban and rural differences within the same region are also substantial in many aspects. Within any regional market, urban consumers' incomes are at least twice as much as those of rural residents, even in the more developed coastal areas. Guangzhou's personal income is five times higher than the poorest town in the same province. The disparities between coastal and inland regions, urban vs. rural areas will remain as the reforms continue to unfold.

In addition to income stratification and regionalism, there are two other notable characteristics of China's consumer market. First, China is still largely a developing country and has been playing "catch up" with other industrialized nations. The consumer market in China seems to have taken the form of "consumption waves," meaning that a particular product is a priority purchase for only a period of time. For instance, color TV was among the first products crazed by Chinese consumers, but soon became unfavored due to saturation and over-production. The waves have been followed by VCRs, washing machines, air conditioners, electric heaters, kitchen appliances, and most recently interior decoration and karaoke machines. As Wong and Maher (1997) have noted, many foreign products have reached the growth or mature stage of the product life cycle in China. Ownership of "traditional" durables, such as color televisions and washing machines, is as high as over 90% in China's urban households, while new products such as microwave ovens and hi-fi stereos only penetrated 20% of the households (Cui 1998). Understanding the mechanics behind China's consumer trends can assist MNCs in making informed and timely decisions about product introduction in China. As MNCs expand into the emerging market areas, they must meet the new success requirements, such as forging closer ties with dealers and establishing a national distribution network.

China's business is extremely subject to the boom and bust cycles. Government policies on foreign investment and climactic conditions that affect harvest can significantly alter the demand for various products. When easy credit mixed with a shortage of supplies led inflation, and buying binges created foreign exchange crises, the Beijing government has in the past retracted some of the reforms, tightened credit and re-centralized foreign trade and investment policy. Understanding this nature of China's developing economy, and constant monitoring of the market environment and political events can help MNCs discover market opportunities, seize them in a timely manner, and avoid becoming a casualty of China's austerity program to cool the country's overheated economy.

In addition to the level of economic development and consumer readiness, the purchase of certain products may be subject to the influence of topographic and climate conditions in various regions. While income exerts a great impact on the purchase of foreign products, ownership of air conditioning equipment is apparently much higher in the South where the climate is hot and humid during the summer. On the other hand, the purchase of cosmetics is higher in the Northeast and Northwest, which have harsh climates. Cosmetics are purchased less frequently in the South where its sub-tropical climate makes wearing cosmetics less feasible (Cui 1998). Thus, understanding the impact of seasonal and climate variations on the purchase of various products can improve marketing planning in terms of promotion and distribution intensity.

DISCUSSION

Contribution of the Research

Any multinational corporation that ignores marketing to a quarter of mankind is putting its future in jeopardy (Xu 1990). Likewise, without fully understanding China's market structure and its consumers, a foreign marketer is risking its long-term viability in the market. This research attempts to delineate the complexity and heterogeneity of Chinese consumers. It provides two meaningful segmentations of the Chinese market. Apart from the singular depiction of Chinese consumers, the research examines simultaneously several important dimensions that influence consumer readiness for the purchase of foreign goods. The demo-psycho-geographic segmentation of Chinese consumers results in four distinctive consumer groups. Their profiles and descriptors provide a realistic understanding of the market potential in each segment, and a useful basis for selecting target market(s) and enacting proper marketing strategies.

Second, segmentation of regional markets focuses on the geographical differences and regional variations in economy, population and local culture. Although these regional differences have been addressed in other circumstances, they have not been considered for marketing strategy implications such as new product introduction, advertising, promotion and distribution. As China has become a major economic force, attracting more foreign retailers, the discrepant level of consumer awareness, and the development in infrastructure such as transportation and communication, present some difficulties in the standardized approach to China. Systematic research of regional variations can help plan for new product introduction, growth and expansion strategies, and overcome the hidden barriers between the regional markets.

Furthermore, this research examines other key notable characteristics of the Chinese consumer market, such as gender and age groups, stage of product life cycle, climate and topographic conditions and seasonal variations. These factors provide further insight into the complexities of the China market. Depending on the product category, marketers can choose the relevant dimensions in segmenting the market and selecting the target segments. Overall, this study presents a good starting point for understanding the diverse consumer groups in China. Today, many MNCs rely on the China market as a significant source of sales and profit, and this dependency is going to continue in the future. As MNCs expand their operations in China and compete with other foreign and domestic firms for consumers' attention, segmentation and targeted marketing will become more relevant.

Suggestions for Future Research

Profiles of these consumer segments are based on review of existing literature and synthesis of secondary data. The merits of the proposed consumer segments and various geographic markets need to be examined with empirical data. Large-scale surveys need to provide updated statistics and can help rectify the validity of the proposed segments and refine their profiles. Such surveys should include all relevant dimensions for market segmentation studies. Other factors that influence consumer readiness such as literacy, family shopping roles and decision making, media usage patterns, consumer perception and attitude, and their impact on advertising and promotion responses, also need to be examined. Longitudinal studies such as the consumer panel by the China Central Viewing and Consulting Center (CVSC), together with the television viewing data, provide rich single-source data (Cui 1998). Essentially, future studies should explore whether these proposed segments exhibit distinctive demographic and psychographic characteristics, and if so, how these differences affect consumers' marketing responses and consumption of various products.

As the Chinese economy and society continue to grow and evolve along many dimensions, China's consumer market will experience dynamic changes. Boundaries of these market segments may shift over time on those key dimensions. Thus, future studies need to provide fresh and reliable data to examine the stability of these proposed segments, update and fine-tune the key characteristics of various segments, and modify the profiles and descriptors. Furthermore, studies of companies that target these consumer segments using differentiated strategies would be helpful to determine the validity of these segmentation frameworks and the effectiveness of their marketing operations.

Given the dynamic political, economic and social environment in China, future studies also need to pay close attention to the development of government policies and their impact on regional economic development and consumer income. Economic inequality can lead to civic discontent and pose a threat to national integrity and social stability. Severe economic disparities among different regions of China may cause political strife and fragmentation of the country. Thus, at issue is whether economy development will further increase the disproportional distribution of wealth between different regions and consumer groups, or will provide opportunity and prosperity for the majority of the Chinese in various regions. Understanding of the dynamic economic and political forces will play a critical role in MNCs' long-term planning and strategies.

Implications for Marketing Strategies

The present research has important implications for MNCs' China marketing strategies, particularly for selection of target market, new production introduction, sales and distribution, and growth and expansion strategies. The common cultural heritage of Chinese consumers may allow certain extent of standardization and coordination in areas such as advertising and human resources management. However, diversity of the China market clearly lends support to differentiated marketing strategies. Discrepant income, various cultures and lifestyles, and the diverse consumption patterns result in different levels of consumer readiness and responsiveness to marketing efforts. The profiles of the four distinctive consumer groups can help firms determine the appropriate target market(s). Depending on the product category, firms can estimate the size of its target market and enact a proper marketing mix.

First, consumer demographics such as income and education largely determine their readiness and frequency of purchase of foreign goods. Depending on the product category and price, MNCs can determine which segment(s) to target. MNCs may then opt to employ the concentrated strategy focusing on a single segment or the differentiated strategy targeting several segments at the same time. Target marketing or the concentrated strategy may well be advised for upscale luxury products. Most sales of imported goods have been centered around large metropolitan areas whose population has high disposable income. Differentiated strategies ought to be adopted if a foreign marketer can deliver a line of products at a full range of quality and price points appealing to several segments. If the product is comparable to those of domestic products, a foreign retailer may want to widen its market by including the *Salary Class*, targeting the add-on and replacement markets. Many products considered inexpensive in the West continue to be a treat for the average urban Chinese family. In this case, a foreign marketer needs to stress quality and value of its products, because these consumers do not have enough money to spend frivolously.

On the other hand, market segmentation does not automatically lead to a differentiated strategy. When some key consumer characteristics are similar across various segments, companies can resort to counter-segmentation or "stitch-niche" market. If the product is an inexpensive consumable item, firms may opt to emphasize its "foreign made" image and appeal to the inter-market segment–the same consumer group across various regional markets. For instance, foreign marketers may target the Yuppies and the youth market in various urban centers across different regional markets. Since most Chinese brands are based at the provincial and municipal level and have a long history, they understand the local markets well and a loyal customer base. Foreign marketers also need to pay more attention to the psychographics as well. They need to devote more resources to studying the motivations and aspirations of various consumer segments and adapt their messages to these segments. For instance, Coca-Cola recently designed a commercial aimed at China's youth market–optimism about the future, yet down-to-earth realism.

The regional variations enumerated above have significant implications for MNCs' entry and expansion strategies and new product introduction. A strategy that initially worked in one region may not automatically translate into success in another region. Thus, companies have to constantly monitor their progress, evaluate and modify their expansion and growth strategies as their businesses grow in China. A "Step by Step, Region by Region" approach to China has become popular with MNCs' planning and marketing strategies. It is crucial for firms entering the market to pick their niche in the context of the local environment and market trends. Foreign firms entering the market are recommended to start with China's biggest cities–Guangzhou, Shanghai and Beijing–which are better in infrastructure, with wealthier and more receptive consumers. As the Chinese say among themselves, "Hong Kong and Taiwan learn from the West; Guangdong learns from Hong Kong and Taiwan; and the rest of China learns from Guangdong." Typically, new products are available in the South and East three to four months ahead of the rest of China. This location allows MNCs to identify the upcoming consumer trends in a timely fashion and respond to the changing needs of consumers rapidly and cost-effectively. Success of a flagship operation in these cities can help prime the market in other cities in the hinterlands. Once firms identify one location as the point of entry, whether it is Guangdong or Shanghai, MNCs can position themselves in any of these markets and strategically use it as a base or springboard for expansion in China. Thus, sequential rather than simultaneous introduction of new products across different regions is more feasible. Consumers in China's prosperous coastal cities are considered the trendsetters and opinion leaders for the rest of China. The "law of retail gravitation" also applies in China, i.e., people in remote and rural areas often go to nearby major cities for purchase of major products.

These regional differences also have implications for sales and distribution strategies. While the sum of opportunities in China is enough to become a driving force for marketing strategies, each individual region has its own distinctive characteristics and contains significant commercial opportunities apart from the others. This diversity warrants a localized approach to marketing planning and strategies. Unilever, for instance, successfully introduced its Wall's Ice Cream in Beijing and Shanghai using different distribution strategies adapted to the local environments. Given China's size and diversity, some MNCs find it makes sense to hire several agents to cover different areas. However, the unique concern and agenda of each regional partnership may jeopardize the effort to coordinate marketing strategies in an already diverse market. As a result, many MNCs are eventually forced to treat each region separately (Batson 1996). For small and medium-sized companies the best course of action is to concentrate on a single regional market. China's distribution networks will continue to evolve along regional lines. As foreign marketers move beyond coastal areas, they will encounter tremendous regional differences, trade barriers and local protectionism. Thus, MNCs need to "plan nationally and act locally"–focusing the overall market trend while paying attention to regional differences.

As China's economy and consumer market continue to evolve, the marketplace will become increasingly fragmented. As MNCs strive to appeal to the divergent needs of various consumer groups, a three-way competition among foreign companies, joint ventures and local firms emerges. Some domestic players are learning quickly the rules of the game and trying to beat the multinationals at their own game. Thus, marketing in China will increasingly resemble its practice in the West. Whether MNCs can establish profitable operations depends on many factors. In-depth understanding of various consumer segments and regional markets can greatly improve the effectiveness of marketing strategies. Successful MNCs' operations will not only contribute to the economic development in China and enhance the quality of life of Chinese consumers, but may also exert tremendous impact on the social and perhaps political progress of the country.

REFERENCES

Aguignier, P. (1988). Regional Disparities Since 1978. In S. Feuchtwang, A. Hussain and T. Pairault (Eds.) *Transforming China's Economy in the Eighties.* Boulder, CO: Westview Press.

Ariga, M., M. Yasue and G. X. Wen (1997). China's Generation III: Viable Target Market Segment and Implications for Marketing Communication. *Marketing and Research Today.* February, 17-24.

Barnett, A. D. (1993). *China's Far West: Four Decades of Change.* Boulder, CO: Westview Press.

Batson, B. (1996). China's Regions: Don't Expect to Find a "National" Market for all Products. *Export Today* 12(4): 22-27.

Clayton, D. (1995). China–Low Incomes Leave Little to Spare. *South China Morning Post*, Oct. 2nd.

Cui, G. (1998). Changing Consumption Patterns Of Chinese Consumers and Marketing Strategy Implications. Forthcoming in the *China International Business Symposium Proceedings.* May, Shanghai, China.

———— (1997). The Changing Faces of the Chinese Consumers. *China Business Review.* July-August, 34-38.

Engel, F. J., H. F. Fiorillo and M. A. Cayley (1972). *Market Segmentation: Concepts and Applications.* New York: Holt.

Europa World Yearbook (1995). Europa Publications, London, United Kingdom.

Garreau, J. (1981). *The Nine Nations of North America.* Boston, Mass: Houghton Mifflin.

Gavin, M. (1994). China's Super Spender. *China Business Review* 21(3), p. 5.

Hamlin, K. (1994). Greater China. *International Business* 7(2): 66-76.

Johnstone, H. (1996). "Little Emperors" Call the Shots. *Asian Business* 32 (9): 67.

Khan, A. R., K. Griffin, C. Risk and R. Zhao (1993). Household Income and Its Distribution in China. In K. Griffin and R. Zhao (Eds.) *The Distribution of Income in China.* St. Martin's Press.

Li, D. and A. M. Gallup (1995). In Search of the Chinese Consumer. *China Business Review* 22(5): 19-22.

Lim, A. C. (1995). Tapping the Retail Market in China. *China Business Review* 22(5): 23-28.

Murray, G. (1994). *Doing Business in China: The Last Great Market.* New York: St. Martin's Press.

Nomani, A. (1993). China Is No. 3 in World Economy. *Wall Street Journal,* May 21st, Sec. 6.

Piturro, M. (1994). Capitalist China? *Brandweek* 35(20): 22-27.

Plummer, J. T. (1974). The Concept and Application of Life Style Segmentation. *Journal of Marketing.* Jan. p. 33.

Rheem, H. (1996). International Investing: Who Profits in China? *Harvard Business Review* 74(1): 10-11.

Sum, Y. L. (1997). The Changing Faces of Chinese Women. *Marketing and Research Today.* February, 25-30.

Wei, R. (1997). Emerging Lifestyles in China and Consequences for Perception of Advertising, Buying Behavior and Consumption Preferences. *International Journal of Advertising* 16(4): 261-275.

Wong, Y. Y. and T. E. Maher (1997). New Key Success Factors for China's Growing Market. *Business Horizon.* May-June, 43-52.

Xu, B. Y. (1990). *Marketing to China: One Billion New Customers.* Lincolnwood, IL: NTC Business Books.

Yeung, Y. M. and X. W. Hu (1992). *China's Coastal Cities.* Honolulu: University of Hawaii Press.

Zhao, R. (1993). Three Features of the Distribution of Income During the Transition to Reform. In K. Griffin and R. Zhao (Eds.). *The Distribution of Income in China.* New York: St. Martin's Press.

Culture and the Fast-Food Marketing Mix in the People's Republic of China and the USA: Implications for Research and Marketing

Patricia M. Anderson

Xiaohong He

SUMMARY. To help multinationals meet consumer needs in the People's Republic of China (PRC), this paper provides basic information about culture and consumer behavior with respect to fast food. A joint effort of researchers from two countries resulted in two PRC surveys and one USA survey using East-, East/West-, and West-influenced instruments, respectively. Results explain the frequency of purchasing fast food and differentiate the segment preferring "fast" from the segment preferring "food" (taste and nutrition), and the younger from the older consumer segment. Results have implications for planning culture-relevant research and marketing mix for similar products and consumers. *[Article copies available for a fee from The Haworth Document Delivery Service: 1-800-342-9678. E-mail address: getinfo@haworthpressinc.com]*

Patricia M. Anderson is Professor of Marketing and Xiaohong He is Associate Professor of International Business and Acting Chair of the Marketing and International Business Department, both at the School of Business, Quinnipiac College, Hamden, CT 06518 USA (E-mail: he@quinnipiac.edu).

The authors thank Tong Wan Shen and Song Dong Yin of Beijing Institute of Business for questionnaires, data collection and data entry; Thomas Kindal for helpful comments and suggestions. The authors would also like to thank Quinnipiac College Faculty Research Committee for grants of research time and funds.

[Haworth co-indexing entry note]: "Culture and the Fast-Food Marketing Mix in the People's Republic of China and the USA: Implications for Research and Marketing." Anderson, Patricia M., and Xiaohong He. Co-published simultaneously in *Journal of International Consumer Marketing* (International Business Press, an imprint of The Haworth Press, Inc.) Vol. 11, No. 1, 1999, pp. 77-95; and: *Consumer Behavior in Asia: Issues and Marketing Practice* (ed: T. S. Chan) International Business Press, an imprint of The Haworth Press, Inc., 1999, pp. 77-95. Single or multiple copies of this article are available for a fee from The Haworth Document Delivery Service [1-800-342-9678, 9:00 a.m. - 5:00 p.m. (EST). E-mail address: getinfo@haworthpressinc.com].

KEYWORDS. Fast food, purchase frequency, consumer segments in USA and PRC

INTRODUCTION

Understanding the relative importance of marketing-mix components, culture/environment influences, and demographics on consumers in Eastern markets is a problem facing Western marketers. This understanding is necessary for almost any type of business marketing products that are relatively mature in developed countries but in the introductory or early life cycle stage of other target countries. Research about PRC consumers can help managers of multinational firms position their products, plan market-segment descriptors and globalize marketing-mix elements (product, price, distribution, promotion).

Because Western fast food has become accessible in the PRC relatively recently, and is presently attracting considerable consumer interest, it is chosen as one example of the difference in the consumer market between the Mao (1949-76) and Deng (1978-97) eras. This paper provides some basic information about norms and values of an Eastern culture, the Peoples' Republic of China (PRC), and also reports on a cooperative East/West consumer research project. Data include three surveys, totaling 1250 respondents. Analyses explain purchase frequency and differentiate the segment preferring "fast" from the segments preferring "food" and the neutrals; and older from younger age segments. Results, reported separately for the three surveys, have culture-related implications for research procedures related to multinational firms' marketing strategy for economies like the PRC.

Both PRC businesses and multinational firms market fast food in the PRC. The research focuses on Western type fast food: pizza, burgers, chicken and other ready-to-eat foods (also beverages) sold at restaurants like Kentucky Fried Chicken, McDonald's and Pizza Hut in the USA and the PRC. The product is a combination of the food and the restaurant chain that sells it. Restaurant chains differentiate themselves in food preparation and/or presentation, for example, "flame broiled, not fried," and "served in a bucket." Consumers either eat fast food in a restaurant or take it away to eat elsewhere. Although fast food is relatively low-priced, fills a basic consumer need and appeals to a wide variety of people, culture/environment and demographics can influence buying behavior, consumer segments, and response to data collection instruments.

The importance of this research is threefold. First, the fast-food market is one of the top seven fastest growing markets in the PRC since economic reform in 1979. Fast food provides not only service, nutrition, and taste that affect a person's health, but also economic values that depend on income growth levels, such as the affordability of eating outside the home or working unit's (danwei's) cheaper cafeterias. In addition, fast food responds to social changes, such as an increasingly fast working pace demanding timesaving service. Second, three surveys conducted during the same period about similar fast-food products and services in Northeast regions of the USA and PRC provide a rich scope for our research. Data were directly collected in the PRC, unlike data collected from foreign Chinese students studying in Western countries, or from Chinese managers in Western training programs. The data are closer to the average PRC consumer in Beijing areas. Third, because increasingly multinational companies have been entering PRC markets, one question frequently asked is: as PRC customers are more exposed to Western foods and services such as Coca-Cola, Pepsi, Big Mac, pizza, and eating at McDonald's and Pizza Hut, will PRC consumers behave more and more like Westerners? What marketing strategies do firms need to adjust in order to adapt successfully in this dynamic and fast changing market?

RELEVANT RESEARCH

Eastern consumers do not necessarily behave like Western consumers (Yau 1994). Western marketers should consider "guo qing," the special situation in China (Yan 1994). Compared with the individualism of American culture, Asian society has a communal tradition. In China, three generations can share a household, and the government has a one-child family policy. Relationships are very important, and building relationships is an ongoing, serious activity (Luk, Fullgrabe and Li 1996). PRC's economic institutions are evolving from a socialistic economy; economic reform and the open-door policy have brought many changes to peoples' lives. The fast pace of economic progress has increased the range of income levels, and changed occupational structure and consumption patterns. Western brands appeared in the PRC in the open-door-policy Deng era (1978 to present), after the 1949-76 Mao era (Xu 1990). "Open to the West" implies that some Western marketers may use marketing mix in selected areas of the PRC so that consumers can learn about and have access to Western products and services.

Fast Food and Consumers

The FCB grid* classifies fast food with low-involvement, "feel" products, along with soaps, snacks, soft drinks, pizza and doughnuts (Ratchford 1987). Fast food seems to fit with low-involvement "transformational"

---

*The model was developed by Richard Vaughn of the Foote, Cone, & Belding Advertising Agency and is commonly known as the FCB grid.

products like candy and regular beer in the Rossiter, Percy and Donovan (1991) advertising planning grid. Low involvement can imply an experienced buyer; however, the entry of a new brand into the category can result in a high-involvement situation (Gensch and Javalgi 1987). The three most important factors in US consumers' deciding where to eat fast food are: time of day, time spent eating (fast service), and price (Harris 1993).

In the United States, families tend to be nuclear, can have more than one child, and tend to have cars for transport. US consumers divide evoked brands of low-cost, frequently-purchased fast food into acceptable (consideration set) and not acceptable. On the average, five fast-food restaurants are in the consideration set (Brown and Wildt 1992). Identification of market segments–bottom-up view–emphasizes the similarity of buyer response to market efforts (Zaltman, LeMasters and Heffring 1982). The Gilly-Enis family life cycle model suggests a relationship between consumption of convenience and junk foods and households with children (Schaninger and Danko 1993). Videophiles, eight percent of US adults, are fast-food consumers, have a fast-paced lifestyle, and watch at least 55 half hours of cable television in an average year (Maxwell 1992). Consumers in different age segments think differently from each other, and like different things because events in formative years make a lasting impression (Schuman and Scott 1989).

Chinese cuisine has a long history, a rich culture, and enjoys worldwide popularity. Because Chinese food takes time to prepare even when cooking time is short, most work units (danwei) serve three inexpensive, relative low-quality meals each day. With economic reform and rising living standards, it has become fashionable and affordable for average PRC consumers to consume more time-saving services and to demand food that is different in taste, culture and quality. As happened earlier in Hong Kong and Singapore, demand for time-saving services is increasing faster than income (Cawing 1971). "Face" ("mianzi," reputation, prestige obtained through one's efforts or conduct) is related to tangible and intangible personal success. Face makes the Chinese risk-averse and slower to accept new products, and more loyal than Westerners once brand image is established (Kindel 1983).

Culture can influence consumers' food choices. The Chinese diet contains more rice, noodles, chicken, pork, vegetables, and fewer sweet desserts compared with an American diet of bread, beef, cheese, dairy products and sweet desserts. Therefore, chicken and beef-noodle fast-food restaurants are more popular in PRC than pizza and burger restaurants. Beef is scarce, and considered very nutritious in traditional Chinese medicine. The older a person is, the more difficult it is to adapt to the new diet. Therefore, older PRC consumers eat burgers for nutrition, and younger consumers eat burgers for taste (e.g., Jimes 1993). Younger persons are more likely to try new foods. Many young, one-child families in urban Beijing take children to McDonald's about once a week. Young Chinese seek novelty and material progress (Lin 1985). Although they do not like pizza, Chinese teens eat at Pizza Hut to be seen; older Chinese like low-fat food; all go to McDonald's to be served, enjoy friends and listen to music (Lu 1994).

The Marketing Mix in USA and PRC

Fast-food restaurants in the USA have drive-through and takeout options, and tend to be surrounded by parking lots. There is more promotional effort in the USA than in the PRC because of the newness of "open to the West" in the PRC and the different interpretation of "competition" in the two countries. In the US, the core age segment for fast food is late teens and age 20s; older consumers are more health conscious. Previously "taste" was advertised; now, nutrition is important (Dodd and Morse 1944). Following the lead of some multinational fast-food marketers, another multinational introduced kids' meals with toys, and free low-fat items for older consumers ("Taco" 1995).

A 1981 PRC field study surveyed 148 middle class (managerial and professional) participants in an executive development program (Thorelli, Fu and Sentell 1986). Respondents believed that advertising provided product information; they avoided risk by buying products popular with their friends. Thorelli, Fu and Sentell (1986) support Kindel's (1983) conclusion that brand and store loyalty in the PRC are high, social risk and word-of-mouth are important, and price competition is nominal.

In the 1980s, Western style food was advertised regularly on radio and television and gained market share in PRC (Lu 1994). The Tiananmen Square incident on June 4, 1989, caused a suspension of foreign advertising. In June, 1990, the Kentucky Fried Chicken restaurant in Tienanmen Square did not advertise, but others were planning advertising campaigns (Geddes 1990). Advertised consumption appeals differed by Eastern country; product performance was the modal appeal in PRC; pleasure, in Hong Kong; and image, in Taiwan (Tse, Belk and Zhou 1989). Magazine ads in the PRC sent messages about product availability, performance and quality (Rice and Lu 1988). Since advertising is still quite new in the PRC, consumers tend not to rely on ads for purchase decisions; however, the ads build brand image. In a high-context culture like the PRC, people look more for what is not being said than for what is being said; if ads persist, people think there is something wrong with the product, and rely on the advice of friends to check whether experience is the same as ad claims.

Fast-food restaurants are popular in Beijing. In the PRC, American fast food is available only in large cities. When KFC first opened in Beijing, it was so prestigious that young couples had their wedding ceremonies in the restaurant. More fast-food chains have entered since that time, and their prices are now considered less expensive than prices of traditional restaurants. With US multinational corporations leading in the PRC fast-food market, local competitors like Ruanhua Chicken and Xiongfi Chicken have entered. In Beijing, Ronghua Chicken serves over 3000 people per day; KFC serves 7000 per day in the Dongsi area. By the end of 1993, there were more than 300 fast-food companies with more than 800 chain restaurants in the PRC. These restaurants are perceived to be nutritious, fast, inexpensive, and clean, using single-use, disposable dishes. Restaurants are classified as Chinese style, Western style, or combination ("New" 1995). Fast-food restaurants are usually located on the first floor of apartment buildings, on bus routes, and accessible from bicycle-parking areas.

Market Segments and International Research

Global teens living in East and West have MTV-inspired consumption patterns. In a recent survey, 54% of US teens and 80% of teens from the Far East said that the USA is the country with the most influence on culture (Miller 1995). Global ads can be used for global segments that exist for certain product categories; these ads are directed at the same audiences in different countries (Hassan & Katsanis 1991). Global print ads for products considered equivalent by consumers in different countries can use local language and "culturally transcendent" meanings, and focus on the Post-modern multicultural segment. For the Post-modern segment born after World War II, television makes the world small, English is widely spoken, and foreign travel is common. Formal and informal eating is associated with social relationships, special occasions and pleasure; gender differences are less marked. Older persons can understand these Post-modern ads less well than younger persons do (Domzal and Kernan 1993).

Consumers in different countries can use the same product for different reasons; a shortcoming of United States research is that it seldom considers research from other countries (Costa and Bamossy 1995). Chinese cultural values should be included in research about the Chinese (Yau 1994). Much cross-cultural marketing research with implications for different countries relies on foreign students (instead of consumers in their own countries) and also on English-language questionnaires (Samiee 1994). Using the same instrument for all subjects can violate equivalence tests in cross-cultural studies (Green and White 1976). It is difficult to find qualified people to do research in China, and to obtain government permission to do surveys. Consumers are relatively unsophisticated, but cooperative if they have a bond with the interviewer. Limited PRC phone distribution (7%) limits phone surveys; there is low response from mail surveys (Miller 1994).

HYPOTHESES AND METHOD

Relevant literature suggests that fast-food consumer behavior is related to demographics, culture/environment, and the marketing mix. It suggests variables and hypotheses for explaining consumption frequency and describing segments. Fast food is a relatively new combination of food preparation, presentation and delivery in both the USA and the PRC, but it is farther along the product life cycle in the former country than in the latter. At present there are rapid economic and social changes in the PRC, and the global marketing effort is relatively new.

Marketing-Mix, Culture/Environment and Demographic Variables

Marketing-mix variables for fast food include: food types eaten, restaurants, quality, advertising, nutrition, taste, price, brand image, restaurant atmosphere and location. Culture/environment variables include: family/friends, everyone does it, save time, save money, enjoy the food, eat with friends, special occasions, traveling, meals and when shopping. Purchase frequency is defined in terms of days per year. Exhibit 1 has operational definitions of variables. Several of these variables connect with Yau's (1994) underlying dimensions of Chinese culture. These are: (1) "group orientation" (family/friends, everyone does it); (2) "continuity" (brand image, purchase frequency); and (3) "face" (price). As in Yau (1994), demographic variables include: age, gender and race. Household size and employment are included because of the one-child family policy and to learn about the extent to which the middle class (see Thorelli, 1986) is represented. Although the Chinese are 95% Han, the Chinese researchers in this study wanted to learn about the minority (non-Han) races.

The three hypotheses in this research state that there are three types of explanatory variables: (1) marketing-mix, (2) the culture/environment influences and (3) demographics that can impact this mix. Because it functions in a cultural and demographic environment, the marketing mix may need changes from region to region to be appropriate for the target market. It is expected that all three types of variables will explain purchase frequency (H1), and distinguish fast-vs.-food (H2) and age (H3) segments in the PRC and the USA. A variable that has explained status in one hypothesis has explanatory status in the others.

Hypotheses About Frequency; and Fast vs. Food and Age Segments

Western fast food is at an earlier stage in the product life cycle in the PRC compared with the USA. It is still a novelty in the PRC, where consumers

EXHIBIT 1. Operational Definitions of Fast-Food Research Variables

Food types consumed. US/PRC1: Check types of fast food you have bought at a fast-food restaurant in the last six months: chicken, burgers, pizza, salad, potatoes (baked, fried, or other), dessert, beverage, other. First six used as dummy variables; PRC1: potatoes are fries only. PRC2: How many types of fast food do you have: 1, 2, over 2; coded 1, 2, 4.

Fast-food restaurants. US/PRC1: check the restaurants in which you bought fast food in the last six months. PRC2: check restaurants having kind of fast food you like. All lists: Kentucky Fried Chicken, McDonald's, Pizza Hut, other. US: Burger King, Wendy's; PRC1: Burger. PRC2: Beef Noodle, Xiongfi Chicken, Ruanhua Chicken, Cafe. For H1-H3, n-1 restaurants were used as dummy variables.

Influences. Family/friends, nutrition, taste, everyone does it. US/PRC1: ads, reduced price, brand image, convenient location; from 5 = very influential to 1 = not at all. PRC2: price, atmosphere; influences are in 3 ranked sets, recoded to 1st, 2nd = 1; 0 = otherwise.

Culture/environment: Save time, save money, enjoy the food, eat with friends. US/PRC1: special occasions, when travelling, for meals (not snacks), for snacks. PRC2: when shopping. Used as separate dummy (0,1) variables.

Purchase frequency. US/PRC1: How often eat food from a fast food restaurant? Coded into days/year: almost daily = 339; once or twice a week = 78; once or twice a month = 18; a few times/year = 6. PRC2: often = 78; occasionally = 18. Explained variable for H1.

Fast vs. food. US/PRC1: a Likert with 5 = strongly agree. "I buy fast food because it is served fast, more than for taste, nutrition." Explained variable for H2: 1-2 recoded to 1; 3 = 2; 4-5 = 3. PRC2: respondents ranking "fast" but not taste/nutrition 1st or 2nd = 3; ranking taste/nutrition but not fast 1st or 2nd = 1; otherwise = 2. See "Influences" above.

Age. US: year of birth–subtract from 1994. PRC1: decade of birth recoded to age decade. PRC2: 16-17, 18-25, 26-35, 36-50, over 50–midpoints. Explained variable for H3: age 16-35, over age 35.

Gender. 0 = male; 1 = female. Answered, but not asked by US phone interviewers.

Race. USA: 1 = white; 0 = other. PRC: 1 = Han; 0 = minority.

Student. USA: 1= fulltime student; 0 = not student. For PRC, see "employed."

Employment. USA: 1 = employed full time. 0 = not. PRC: recoded to employed = 1, student = 0.

Number of persons in household, including respondent. US/PRC1: open-ended. PRC2: below 3, 3-5, above 5, recoded to 2, 4, 6.

require time both to access restaurants and to be served (excess demand causes lines). Culture, environment and demographics can require a different marketing-mix in early versus later product life cycle, and even alter marketing-mix influence. Frequency of buying Western-type fast food can be based not only on the marketing mix, but also on culture/environment and demographics. Therefore, we test H1 to learn which variables explain purchase frequency, ranging from heavy to light usage.

> H1: For consumers of Western-type fast food, marketing-mix, culture/ environment and demographic variables explain purchase frequency.

A question arises as to whether people buy fast food because it is "food" to be valued for taste or nutrition, or because it is served fast. Fast-food marketers can target the "fast" segment, the "food" segment and even the neutral segment of consumers, who prefer neither fast nor taste but buy the food. Marketers have the opportunity to use marketing mix to persuade the neutrals towards "fast" or towards "food," and/or to satisfy both "fast" and the "food." Knowing the relative impact of culture/environment, demographics and marketing-mix variables can help Western multinationals determine how to deploy the fast-food marketing mix effectively, especially when entering Eastern markets where "taste" preferences can vary from those in Western markets. Taste is an affect variable; one can like or dislike a particular taste for individual subjective reasons. Nutrition is a cognitive variable; one can believe that a certain food is nutritious and that nutrition benefits health. Taste and nutrition are associated with food; fast is associated with service. Therefore, we test H2.

> H2: For consumers of Western-type fast food, marketing-mix, culture/ environment and demographic variables discriminate the segment preferring "fast" from the segment preferring "food" (taste/ nutrition) and the neutral segment.

The United States is a youth-oriented society of individuals. Old and young tend to have some behaviors in common because the old consider themselves youthful. The relatively modest size of fast-food meals suits older USA consumers who do not need or want larger meals. In the PRC, governed by the Confucius culture, older age is commonly associated with wisdom and internal character; and behavior is associated with societal influence (Moran and Harris 1990). A change in government policy from Mao to Deng is most likely to cause a difference in behavior of PRC consumers age 35 and under compared with those over age 35 because the younger group was not alive during the Mao regime, and the older group was first influenced by Mao.

There was no such government policy change in the USA. Children under 16 are excluded because they are less able to respond to all questionnaire questions.

> H3: For consumers of Western fast food, marketing-mix, culture/environment and demographic variables discriminate the consumer segment age 16-35 from the segment over age 35.

Method

After USA and PRC colleagues had agreed on the product types, information to be collected, questions, and sampling/survey guidelines, the PRC colleagues prepared a self-administered questionnaire, written in Chinese characters. This PRC2 questionnaire was designed for the traditional PRC percentage-type analysis. Because the traditional percentage analysis does not provide for relationships among variables, the USA and PRC1 questionnaires were designed mainly by the US researchers with the original version written in English for multivariate analyses, regression (H1, frequency), and discriminant analyses (H2, fast vs. food; and H3, age segments). The bilingual, bicultural author, who besides other research work analyzed country-specific implications and data, translated language and culture.

Using cluster sampling in communities/neighborhoods in Beijing and surrounding areas, a community official distributed and collected questionnaires in apartment buildings housing workers from several work units. Interviewers contacted respondents in work-unit housing selected from nine areas in and around Beijing in northeast PRC in two separate spring, 1995, surveys: PRC2, followed weeks later by PRC1. US data were collected in fall, 1995, by phone survey from a supervised room in a Polling Institute in northeastern United States using a random sample of telephone numbers from an entire state, and three callbacks to reach a given phone number.

An issue in this research is the extent to which Western research procedures can be used in Eastern countries. When research methods developed in one culture are applied to another without adapting for cultural differences throughout the research, results can be misleading. For example, the PRC has experienced a leadership change from Mao's command economy to Deng's more market-oriented economy, beginning in 1978. Is this change, with resulting economic and social developments, associated with differences in behavior of the younger versus the older consumers? Are results for Western-influenced research the same as for Eastern-influenced research for the younger and older age groups?

RESULTS AND DISCUSSION

Response rates were 90% for the PRC and 67% for the USA. After deleting incomplete responses, there were 290, 173, and 797 responses for the USA, PRC1 and PRC2 surveys respectively. Data received from the PRC on disk were recoded in the USA as explained in Exhibit 1. Demographics compare favorably with population percentages (see Lee 1994 and "Population" 1995). The PRC2 questionnaire was specifically designed for percentage-type analysis. Columns 1-3 of Table 1 are consistent with the traditional PRC percentage-type analysis, and also contain means.

In Table 1, a larger percentage of US and PRC1 respondents eat fast food to save time than to save money; the reverse is true for PRC2 respondents. In the Table 1, 47% PRC2, 5% PRC1, and 49% USA respondents consider price influence important; 42% PRC2, 51% PRC1, 58% USA consider taste important; 20% PRC2, 47% PRC1 and 16% USA consider nutrition important. PRC2 (67%) respondents eat at Beef Noodle restaurants. PRC2 (52%), 46% PRC1 and 37% USA respondents eat at Kentucky Fried Chicken; 42% PRC2, 43% PRC1 and 78% USA respondents eat McDonald's fast food. Family/ friends' influence was important to 19% of PRC2 respondents, compared with 32% of PRC1 and 23% of US respondents. Other non-marketing-mix influences included: save time: 44% PRC2, 38% PRC2, 75% USA; and enjoy the food: 59% PRC2, 49% PRC1, and 64% USA. PRC colleagues omitted advertising from the PRC2 fast food questionnaires because they did not consider advertising important for fast food, but added atmosphere. Atmosphere was important to 29% of PRC2 respondents.

Of PRC2 respondents, 70% eat fast food occasionally, modal household income is 200-400 renminbi ($50 or less) per month, modal household size is 3-5 people, and respondents consume about two types of fast food on the average (compared with five types for US respondents). Respondents to both PRC questionnaires included about the same percentages of workers (23), peasants (2), teachers (10), soldiers (3), students (15), and entrepreneurs (5). PRC2 had a higher percentage of "other" (8 versus 15); PRC1 had a higher percentage of cadres (39 vs. 23). Chinese respondents are younger on the average: PRC2 (32 years), PRC1 (37 years), and USA (42 years).

Because variables in the PRC2 instrument were operationally defined to fit the traditional PRC percentage analysis, and the USA and PRC1 instruments were designed for multivariate analysis, robust results are most likely to be found in the most important variables, defined for H1 as the five variables for each survey having the largest standardized regression coefficients, and for H2 and H3 as the five with both the largest discriminant loadings and standardized canonical discriminant function coefficients. Columns 4-6 of Table 1 contain regression results for the test of H1, explaining purchase frequency. Explanatory power is greatest for PRC1 (column 5, R-square = .41),

TABLE 1. Percentages, Means and Significant Standardized Regression Coefficients (Explaining Fast-Food Purchase Frequency: USA and PRC*)

Explanatory variables	Percentages			Regression Coefs.		
	USA	PRC1	PRC2	USA	PRC1	PRC2
Column	(1)	(2)	(3)	(4)	(5)	(6)
Marketing Mix:						
Food Types:						.08b
Chicken	62.1	55.6	n.a.		.17b	n.a.
Burgers	80.0	31.4	n.a.		−.12c	n.a.
Pizza	75.2	24.3	n.a.			n.a.
Salad	51.4	34.0	n.a.		.13c	n.a.
Potatoes	81.4	30.8	n.a.			n.a.
Dessert	21.0	23.7	n.a.		.23a	n.a.
Restaurants:						
McDonald's	78.3	42.6	42.2			.11a
Kentucky Fried Chicken	36.9	46.2	52.4	.27a	−.19b	.06b
Pizza Hut	35.5	21.3	9.7	−.10c		.10a
Burger King	56.6	n.a.	n.a.			n.a.
Wendy's	38.6	n.a.	n.a.		n.a.	n.a.
Beef Noodle	n.a.	n.a.	66.6	n.a.	n.a.	
Xiongfi Chicken	n.a.	n.a.	13.6	n.a.	n.a.	.09a
Ruanhua Chicken	n.a.	n.a.	11.4	n.a.	n.a.	.08a
Cafe	n.a.	n.a.	20.2			
Influences:						
Advertising	22.4	25.4	n.a.	−.11b		n.a.
Nutrition	15.9	47.4	19.7			
Taste	58.3	50.9	42.2		−.15c	
Atmosphere	n.a.	n.a.	29.2			
Price	49.3	5.2	47.5	.17a		−.11a
Brand image	24.5	30.6	n.a.		.19b	n.a.
Convenient location	76.6	34.5	n.a.		.20b	n.a.
Culture/Environment:						
Family, friends	23.4	32.3	19.0		.18b	
Everyone does it	18.3	9.2	26.0	.12b		
Save time	74.8	37.6	43.9			
Save money	21.4	9.8	61.7	.14a	.24a	
Enjoy the food	64.1	49.1	58.5			
Eat with friends	45.2	25.4	32.0			
Special occasions						
Travelling	92.1	28.9	n.a.		−.16b	n.a.
Meals	77.6	37.0	n.a.	.12b		n.a.
When Shopping	n.a.	n.a.	27.2	n.a.	n.a.	

Explanatory variables Column	Percentages			Regression Coefs.		
	USA (1)	PRC1 (2)	PRC2 (3)	USA (4)	PRC1 (5)	PRC2 (6)
Demographics						
Age (1 = over 35)	61	51	34	−.18b		−.06c
Gender (1 = female)	53	46	57			
Race (1 = white/Han)	82	83	93	−.14b		
Student (1 = yes)	14	14	16			
Employed (1 = yes)	66	85	83			
	Means (and Std. Dev.)					
Number in household	3 (1)	4 (1)	3 (1)			−.09a
Purchase Frq. (Days/Yr.)	57 (75)	31 (60)	32 (75)	(dependent variable)		

*See Exhibit 1 for definitions of variables; regressions omit cafe, beverages.

compared with USA (column 4, R-square = .25) and PRC2 (column 6, R-square = .13. The Exhibit-1 definition of frequency shows that PRC2 has only two categories compared with the five categories used for the USA and PRC1. Significant regression coefficients include both cultural and demographic variables, for example: "everyone does it" for the USA, and "save money" and household size for PRC2. These and other variables in the top five suggest marketing-mix strategies. For example: significance of brand image, saving money, and price influence suggest ad messages and pricing opportunities. Also, KFC (USA), dessert and not-KFC (PRC1), and McDonald's and Pizza Hut (PRC2) indicate products and restaurants associated with frequent buying. Mealtime (USA) and convenient location (PRC1) suggest other reasons that could be promoted for consuming fast food frequently. Although regression results in columns 4-6 of Table 1 suggest different specifics, they contain information that can be used for product, price, place and/or promotion. Results support H1 for the marketing mix and culture/environment, but minimally for demographics.

For fast-vs.-food (H2) and age (H3) hypotheses respectively, Table 2 contains discriminant loadings (structure matrices) for the top five variables. Loadings are pooled-within-group correlations between discriminating variables and canonical discriminant functions. A larger loading indicates a higher correlation. Discriminant loadings for H2 are in columns 1-3 of Table 2. Product, place and price separate consumers who prefer "fast" from those who prefer "food." Group means indicate which segment has the larger mean. The USA fast segment wants to save time in a convenient location, and has a large percentage of whites and Burger King customers; the food segment values nutrition more. More respondents of the PRC1 food segment

TABLE 2. Discriminant Loadings for USA and PRC "Fast" Segments and Age Segments*

Explanatory Variables	"Fast" vs. "Food"			≤ Age 35 vs. > Age 35		
	USA	PRC1	PRC2	USA	PRC1	PRC2
Marketing Mix:						
No. Food Types Consumed:			.00			−.32
Chicken	.05	.18	n.a.	.02	.12	n.a.
Burgers	.12	.13	n.a.	.22	.28	n.a.
Pizza	−.22	−.05	n.a.	.13	.06	n.a.
Salad	−.07	.06	n.a.	.01	.17	n.a.
Potatoes	.08	−.13	n.a.	.28	.13	n.a.
Dessert	−.16	−.00	n.a.	.03	.11	n.a.
Restaurant Brands Chosen:						
McDonald's	.11	−.02	−.05	.01	.06	−.07
Kentucky Fried Chicken	.00	.20	−.02	−.07	.28	.07
Pizza Hut	−.01	.06	.05	.25	.20	−.16
Burger King	.25	n.a.	n.a.	.19	n.a.	n.a.
Wendy's		n.a.	n.a.		n.a.	n.a.
Beef Noodle	n.a.	n.a.	−.13	n.a.	n.a.	.14
Xiongfi Chicken	n.a.	n.a.	.03	n.a.	n.a.	−.08
Ruanhua Chicken	n.a.	n.a.	.01	n.a.	n.a.	−.08
Influences:						
Advertising	.07	.28	n.a.	.00	.24	n.a.
Nutrition	−.23	.54	.38	−.06	.33	−.14
Taste	−.18	.67	.62	.30	.25	−.17
Atmosphere	n.a.	n.a.	−.20	n.a.	n.a.	.06
Price	.05	.30	−.32	.19	.31	.16
Brand image	−.09	.08	n.a.	.02	.27	n.a.
Convenient location	.47	.16	n.a.	.00	.43	n.a.
Culture/Environment:						
Family, friends	.00	.33	.00	.15	.25	.00
Everyone does it	.06	.29	.04	.23	.26	−.15
Save time	.47	−.03	−.24	.03	−.03	−.11
Save money	.04	.08	−.10	.06	.16	.16
Enjoy the food	−.04	.44	.01	−.02	.13	.14
Eat with friends	.08	−.14	.14	.42	−.02	−.04
Special occasions	−.14	−.10	.06	.06	.02	−.02
Travelling	.06	.16	n.a.	−.07	.15	n.a.
Meals (not snacks)	−.10	.30	n.a.	.20	.06	n.a.
When shopping	n.a.	n.a.	.09	n.a.	n.a.	−.02
Prefer fast to taste	dependent variable			−.06	−.10	.16
Purchase frequency	.05	−.06	.01	.11	.20	−.28

Explanatory Variables	"Fast" vs. "Food"			≤ Age 35 vs. > Age 35		
	USA	PRC1	PRC2	USA	PRC1	PRC2
Demographics						
Age	−.11	−.08	−.10	dependent variable		
Gender (1 = female)	−.04	.02	.10	.08	.12	−.33
Race (1 = white/Han)	.33	−.01	.03	−.14	.12	−.01
Student (1 = yes)	.08	**	**	.38	**	**
Employed (1 = yes)	.04	−.11	−.06	−.16	−.51	.70
Number in household	.04	−.04	.02	.25	−.08	.34
% correctly classified	59	64	92	70	83	67
Number of observations	290	173	797	290	173	797

* Underlining means that the variable is in the discriminant function.
**See operational definition in Exhibit 1.

compared with the fast segment value taste and nutrition, eat meals not snacks, enjoy the food, and eat at KFC (Beijing did not have a Burger King at the time of the survey). The PRC2 fast segment not only wants to save time, but also is influenced by atmosphere and price; the food segment is influenced by taste and nutrition. Results support H2. Percentages correctly classified in the fast-vs.-food analyses were 72% for PRC2, 64% for PRC1 and 59% for USA.

Analyses for H3 are in columns 4-6 of Table 2. For USA data, the younger group has larger households, more students, more taste-influence, and a higher proportion of persons who eat fast food with friends and like potatoes. The younger PRC1 group contains fewer employed and is more influenced by convenient location, family/friends, nutrition and price. The younger PRC2 group has more females and smaller households, buys more often, and eats more food types. Results support H3 for marketing mix, culture/environment and demographics. Percentages correctly classified were 67% for PRC2, 83% for PRC1 and 70% for USA.

IMPLICATIONS AND FUTURE RESEARCH

Implications for Marketing Mix

The environment of fast economic development and social/cultural changes in China leads to a rising living standard for PRC consumers, and a greater opportunity for multinational firms to serve this market. With the evolution of a true consumer's market taking shape in the PRC, a contribution of this study will help firms to position and design a market mix and to select a market segment. Fast-food products like KFC's chicken and McDonald's burgers have adapted well to the traditional Chinese-cultural diet because chicken and beef are known in the PRC for their nutritious content in traditional Chinese medicine. The fast-food concept that fits the US fast life style has adapted successfully to PRC's consumers' life style, because less waiting and fast service do not mean to eat fast. The results imply multiple-behavior segments: the "fast" segment can differ from the "food" segment; the older age segment can differ from the younger segment. These results indicate these market segments behave differently.

Marketing-mix variables predominate in results for hypotheses 1-3, although different specific variables are in the top five in different surveys. While product, price, and place variables are in the top five, they, and also the culture/environment and demographic variables, contain information that marketers can use to target chosen segments and to increase patronage. For example, promote convenient location, saving time, and atmosphere to the "fast" US, PRC1 and PRC2 segments respectively. It is important for multinational companies to recognize that several variables rather than a dominant one can influence consumer behavior, and also to understand the impacts of social and economic development stages on consumer behavior. With 1.2 billion people, the PRC is a very large market, largely untapped, with high economic growth. There exists a large number of potential customers to be reached with effective marketing strategies. Even one target behavior and/or age segment can be large enough to be profitable.

Results also suggest that researchers should continuously monitor developments in the rapidly changing PRC. Westerners doing research in the PRC should be aware that data collection instruments prepared for Western multivariate analysis and adapted for research in the PRC can have results different from those prepared for PRC percentage-type analysis. The difference suggests that marketers consider the most important variables in each survey and study the effects of variables from both sets when planning marketing mix, positioning and segmentation. Further, for example, in PRC-colleagues-designed questionnaire and US-researchers-designed ones (for PRC and US markets respectively) worked out from the same research plan, the importance and analysis methods may differ in details due to a need of adapting to a specific local situation. For example in Exhibit 1, the PRC-designed questionnaire (PRC2) and the US-designed questionnaires (PRC1 and USA) used different operational definitions of some variables. Also Table 2 shows that US-designed questionnaires included the advertising variable but not atmosphere; the reverse was true for the PRC questionnaire (PRC2). Without considering cross-cultural factors, the researchers may overlook and even miss some important information.

Limitations and Suggestions for Future Research

Results in Tables 1 and 2 are valid only for similar consumers in similar regions and similar time periods. Researchers must look beyond both their own countries' theories and respondents from other countries who live outside their home countries. It is essential to conduct research with the help of someone who thoroughly understands the language and culture in the country researched. Speaking a common language does not guarantee that two people from different countries communicate effectively. A knowledge of the culture is needed to understand the extent to which the same words have different meanings in different cultures.

Although the three survey instruments were designed according to an agreed upon master plan, and the PRC1 instrument was a second attempt to design a comparable instrument, differences still remained. On the one hand, the PRC2 instrument included variables not in the original agreement. On the other hand, it was probably a closer fit to the PRC situation which has some important variables, like "beef noodle" not relevant in USA, but very relevant in PRC.

The conclusion in this paper is applicable to future research in the West about the PRC, to pay considerable attention to cultural interpretations of words and marketing behaviors. This type of consumer-behavior research should be ongoing in the future because product life cycle stages can change, and worldwide communications can increase similarities among target consumers in different regions and countries. These changes can require adjustments in research methods and in product, price, place and promotion strategies.

REFERENCES

Brown, Juanita J. and Albert R. Wildt (1992), "Consideration Set Measurement," *Journal of the Academy of Marketing Science*, 20 (Summer), 235-243.

Cawing, Tong-yung (1991), *The Impacts of Industrialization upon Consumption Patterns with Special Reference to Hong Kong and Singapore*, Hong Kong: Economic Research Center, Hong Kong Series–Occasional Papers 2. The Chinese University of Hong Kong.

Costa, Janeen A. and Gary J. Bamossy, eds. (1995), *Marketing in a Multicultural World*, Thousand Oaks, CA: Sage.

Dodd, Tim H. and Steve Morse (1994), "The Impact of Media Stories Concerning Health Issues on Food Product Sales," *Journal of Consumer Marketing*, 11 (2), 17-24.

Domzal, Teresa J. and Jerome B. Kernan (1993), "Mirror, Mirror: Some Post-modern Reflections on Global Advertising," *Journal of Advertising*, 22 (December), 1-20.

Geddes, Andrew (1990), "Ads Return to Chinese Market," *Advertising Age*, 61 (June 4), 41.

Gensch, Dennis H. and R. G. Javalgi (1987), "The Influence of Involvement on Disaggregate Attribute Choice Models," *Journal of Consumer Research*, 14 (1), 71-82.

Green, Robert T. and Phillip D. White (1976), "Methodological Considerations in Cross-National Consumer Research," *Journal of International Business Studies*, 7 (Fall-Winter), 81-87.

Harris, John (1990), "I Don't Want Food, I Want Fast," *Forbes*, 146 (Oct. 1), 186.

Hassan, Salah S. and Lea P. Katsanis (1991), "Identification of Global Consumer Segments: A Behavioral Framework," *Journal of International Consumer Marketing*, 3 (2), 11-28.

Jimes, Jeffrey (1993), *Consumption and Development*, New York: St. Martin's Press.

Kindel, Thomas I. (1983), "A Partial Theory of Chinese Consumer Behavior: Marketing Strategy Implications," *Hong Kong Journal of Business Management*, v. 1.

Lee, Hessler (1994), *Profile of China Markets: Complete Market Data on Spending Pattern of 1.1 Billion Consumers in China*. B.C. Canada: Hercules Publishing House.

Lin, Pin-hsien (1985), *Consumer Behavior*. Beijing: Electronics Industry Publisher.

Lu, Hui (1994), "China's Great Gastronomical Revolution," *China Today*, (April), 15-17. (August 27), 50-51.

Luk, S.T.K., L. Fullgrave and S.C.Y. Li (1996), "Influences of Chinese Culture on Creating and Maintaining Relationships with Customers: Implications for Effective Direct Selling," Polytechnic University of Hong Kong, manuscript, 25 pp.

Maxwell, Robert (1992), "Videophiles and Other Americans," *American Demographics*, 14 (July), 48-55.

Miller, Cyndee (1994), "China Emerges as Latest Battleground for Marketing Researchers," *Marketing News*, 28 (February 14), 1, 2.

———— (1995), "Teens Seen as the First Truly Global Consumers," *Marketing News*, 29 (3/27), 9.

Moran, R. and P. R. Harris (1990), *Managing Cultural Differences*. Gulf Publishing Company.

"New Trade on the City Street: Fast Food and Food Delivery" (1995), *People's Daily* (October 12), 3.

"Population and Retail Sales by Store Group, 1994," *Sales & Marketing Management*, C24-C26; S&MM Estimates published on January 1, 1995.

Ratchford, Brian T. (1987), "New Insights about the FCB Grid," *Journal of Advertising Research*, 27 (4), 24-38.

Rice, M. D. and Z. Lu (1988), "A Content Analysis of Chinese Magazine Ads," *Journal of Advertising*, 17: 43-48.

Rossiter, John R., Larry Percy and Robert J. Donovan (1991), "A Better Advertising Planning Grid," *Journal of Advertising Research*, (October/November), 11-21.

Samiee, Saeed (1994), "Customer Evaluation of Products in a Global Market," *Journal of International Business Studies*, 25 (No. 3), 579-604.

Schaninger, Charles M. and William D. Danko (1993), "A Conceptual and Empirical Comparison of Alternative Household Life Cycle Models," *Journal of Consumer Research*, 19 (March), 580-94.

Schuman, Howard and Jacqueline Scott (1989), "Generations and Collective Memories," *American Sociological Review*, 54 (June), 359-381.

"Taco Bell Seeks Multiple Markets with Kids' Meals, 'Border Lights'"(1995), *Marketing News*, 29 (August 14), 5.

Thorelli, Hans B., Fu Shenzhao, and Gerald D. Sentell (1986), "The Middle Class and the Marketplace: The PRC, Overseas Chinese, and Thailand," in S. Tamer Cavusgil, ed. *Advances in International Marketing*, Greenwich, CT: JAI Press, 143-178.

Tse, David K., Russell W. Belk and Nan Zhou (1989), "Becoming a Consumer Society: A Longitudinal and Cross-Cultural Content Analysis of Print Ads from Hong Kong, the People's Republic of China and Taiwan," *Journal of Consumer Research*, 15 (March), 457-472.

"U.S. Marketing Plans Are Churning in China" (1994), *Advertising Age*, 65 (Sept. 5), 38.

Xu Bai Yi (1990), *Marketing to China*, Lincolnwood, IL: NTC Business Books.

Yan, Rick (1994), "To Reach China's Consumers, Adapt to Guo Qing," *Harvard Business Review*, (September/October), 66-74.

Yau, Oliver Hon Ming (1994), *Consumer Behavior in Asia*, NY: Routledge.

Zaltman, Gerald, Karen LeMasters and Michael Heffring (1982), *Theory Construction in Marketing*, New York: Wiley.

Influence of Chinese Cultural Values on Consumer Behavior: A Proposed Model of Gift-Purchasing Behavior in Hong Kong

Oliver H. M. Yau
T. S. Chan
K. F. Lau

SUMMARY. Gift giving is often a highly visible social behavior which individuals perform among family members and social or business friends. The importance of the symbolism of gifts would suggest that social referents may affect the purchase decisions for gifts. One's social referents are often determined by one's cultural background or affiliation. We propose that the behavior of gift giving among Hong Kong consumers is mediated by such Chinese cultural values as face saving, reciprocity and *guanxi* (relationship). This paper summarizes the literature on Chinese cultural values and then develops a more parsimonious model to explain the influence of Chinese cultural values on gift giving. Propositions are developed based on this comprehensive model for future testing. *[Article copies available for a fee from The Haworth Document Delivery Service: 1-800-342-9678. E-mail address: getinfo@haworthpressinc.com]*

KEYWORDS. Chinese cultural values, model building, gift-purchasing behavior in Hong Kong

Oliver H. M. Yau is Associate Dean and Chair Professor of Marketing, Faculty of Business, City University of Hong Kong. T. S. Chan is Dean, Faculty of Business and Chair Professor of Marketing, and K. F. Lau is Associate Professor of Marketing and International Business, both at Lingnan College, Hong Kong.

[Haworth co-indexing entry note]: "Influence of Chinese Cultural Values on Consumer Behavior: A Proposed Model of Gift-Purchasing Behavior in Hong Kong." Yau, Oliver H. M., T. S. Chan, and K. F. Lau. Co-published simultaneously in *Journal of International Consumer Marketing* (International Business Press, an imprint of The Haworth Press, Inc.) Vol. 11, No. 1, 1999, pp. 97-116; and: *Consumer Behavior in Asia: Issues and Marketing Practice* (ed: T. S. Chan) International Business Press, an imprint of The Haworth Press, Inc., 1999, pp. 97-116. Single or multiple copies of this article are available for a fee from The Haworth Document Delivery Service [1-800-342-9678, 9:00 a.m. - 5:00 p.m. (EST). E-mail address: getinfo@haworthpressinc.com].

97

INTRODUCTION

Chinese are inveterate gift givers as gifts express friendship and can symbolize hopes for a good future relationship, a successful conclusion of an endeavor, generosity, or appreciation for a favor done. Because of the symbolic meanings of gift giving, it is important that gift givers select the most appropriate presents. Favors should be rewarded materially even though symbolic values, in terms of thoughtfulness, often weigh more than simple monetary value. That is, the most expensive gift is not always the appropriate gift.

Accepting or rejecting a gift that has been offered has also a symbolic meaning. The gift receiver may not want to be in the giver's debt or have no intention of establishing a *guanxi* (relationship) with the giver. In most of the cases, if someone presents another one with a gift, the receiver is expected to reciprocate in kind or through a favor.

Hong Kong is an important trading and financial center located on the southern coast of China. Hong Kong is a sophisticated and highly educated society of 6.3 million people. After over 150 years of British rule, Hong Kong was reverted back to Chinese sovereignty as a Special Administrative Region of the People's Republic of China on July 1, 1997. Ninety-five percent of the Hong Kong people are of Chinese descent. For most people in Hong Kong, Chinese cultural values are important influences over one's behavior in life. Thus, relating Chinese cultural values to purchase behavior can be an effective avenue for understanding consumer behavior. The behavior of gift purchasing is among the most frequently mentioned social activities among Chinese people. But how do we explain the motivation behind gift purchasing? What factors affect the nature and value of a gift? How would *guanxi* (relationship) between giver and receiver of the gift influence the purchase decision? In an effort to understand better the gift-buying behavior, this study relates the Chinese cultural values of face, *guanxi*, and reciprocity with gift-purchasing behavior. The purpose of this study is to apply the theory of reasoned action in evaluating the influence of Chinese cultural values on the gift-purchasing behavior of Hong Kong consumers. A proposed model was developed to illustrate the issue. The behavioral modelling approach employed attempts to provide an opportunity to relate the strength and significance of different Chinese cultural values on the shopping behaviors.

CULTURAL VALUES AND GIFT GIVING

Culture can be defined as an evolving system of concepts, values and symbols inherent in a society–a learned system of behavior that organises experience, determines an individual's position within social structures and guides actions in a multitude of situations, both known or unknown. The usefulness of culture and other anthropological tools for analysing business systems is widely acknowledged in many international business studies.

A culture is a group of people sharing common beliefs, norms and customs. It influences one's behavior toward family, friends, work, education, consuming and other important concepts and processes. The Chinese cultural values, as identified by Bond (1989), can be applied to improve understanding of Chinese consumer behavior. For instance, Chinese cultural values can be used as an effective basis for market segmentation and positioning (Yau 1994a). Social referent influence is significant in determining an individual's shopping behavior (Ryan 1982). The visible nature of gift giving and the importance of social interaction implications support a proposition that cultural values are likely to influence shopping behavior.

Chinese cultural values can be used as strong predictors for shopping behaviors among Hong Kong people, such as gift purchasing and gift giving. Face involves an individual's perception of social feedback on his/her self-presentation. The negotiation between an individual and the society may influence the person's behavior due to the need for face. Face is a type of other-directed self esteem (Chow and Ho 1992). Because of the perceived threat of losing face, an individual might worry about his/her own goodness or self ego and thus have a feeling of *ch'i* (shame) (Yang 1991, Baumeister 1986, Tedeschi 1986).

The level of *guanxi* (or tie) in dyadic relationships is vital to understanding face and shame (Yang 1992). *Guanxi* influences the ability of an individual to reach an equilibrium where aspired face equals estimated face. Face gain or loss will influence an individual's self image, resulting in improved or worsened *guanxi*. With improved *guanxi*, the relative strength of human obligation and moral values becomes greater, whereas when *guanxi* worsens, an individual's perceived importance of materialistic values becomes greater. That is why doing favors can lead to indebtedness or reciprocity.

Gift giving is a form of reciprocity. When the giver is doing a favor, such as presenting a gift, the receiver becomes indebted to the giver if the gift is accepted. If the receiver reciprocates with a gift, the original giver will also be indebted (Sahlins 1965). Gift giving is also a type of face act, as gift giving is a tool for enhancing interpersonal relationships. When consumers are making the choice regarding gift selection and involvement in the product and the buying task (gift purchasing), face, *guanxi*, and reciprocity will all be playing important roles in determining behaviors.

In summary, the need to reciprocate often prompts the need for gift giving. The consumer decision process in a gift-purchasing situation (motivated by the desire to gain face) may be influenced by the perceived risk of losing face and the level of *guanxi* between the giver and the receiver.

CHINESE CULTURAL VALUES

Researchers in the study of Chinese cultural values may find it surprising to learn that Chinese values form a clear and consistent system throughout generations (Kindle 1982, Hsu 1970). In terms of the ways Chinese cultural values are classified, various scholars have adopted different approaches. Wright (1970) describes the Chinese culture with a system of thirteen values while Yau (1988, 1994b) uses Kluckhohn and Strodtbeck's (1961) classification and proposes a new classification of twelve Chinese cultural values. In fact, Wright's approach is very similar to Yau's. However, Yau's approach is more structured and is connected to recent developments in management and marketing studies in the West.

There are other cultural value systems in the literature, which are mostly the result of Western observations. Parsons and Shils (1951) claim that all human action is determined by five cultural values such as effectively, self-orientation, universalism, ascription and specificity. Inkeles and Levinson (1954) summarize three cultural values that they label 'standard analytic issues': relation to authority, self-conception, and primary conflicts and the ways of dealing with them. Hofstede (1980) classifies related work-values into four dimensions: power distance, uncertainty avoidance, individualism and masculinity. His dimensions are quite similar to those of Inkeles and Levinson (1954). Hofstede's classification has been widely used for cross-cultural comparison because of its readiness and ease for use. However, his classification is either too succinct to be used in studies that deal with consumer behavior and other micro-phenomena leading to managerial implications, or it lacks both face and content validation. For example, many authors argue that individualism is essentially alien to the Asian ethos (Ho 1976, 1979, 1988; Hsu 1971). The measure of individualism may then be invalid or its inclusion may be meaningless.

Definitely, there are more than four major values, which can be used to describe or interpret Chinese behavior. Omission of some other variables such as *yuan* (fate) and *bao* (reciprocity) makes the classification meaningless and irrelevant to the Chinese culture. Any attempt to adopt Hofstede's dimensions in Chinese culture-related research will lead to biased and incomplete findings. Along the same lines, Bond and Hofstede (1989) added a fifth dimension, Confucian dynamics, to Hofstede's original classification. Unfortunately, this addition does not contribute to the explanation of Chinese business behaviors or psychology according to Chinese poetry literature, as the items contributing to Confucian dynamics virtually do not pertain purely to this dimension at all. This indicates their misunderstanding of the Chinese philosophies that provide the foundation for the development of Chinese cultural values. In this study, we therefore adopt some of the Chinese cultural values identified by Yau (1988, 1994a) that relate more directly to gift giving.

The Concept of Face (mien-tsu and lien). Chinese are acutely sensitive to having and maintaining face in all aspects of social and business life. Face can be classified into two types: *lien* and *mien-tsu. Lien* represents the 'confidence of society in the integrity of the ego's moral character, the loss of which makes it impossible for him to function properly within the community' (Hu 1944). *Mien-tsu* stands 'for the kind of prestige life, through success and ostentation' (Hu 1994). Those two types of face have a particular implication on gift giving. On the one hand, people will lose *lien* (*du lien*) when presenting a gift that does not match their status or the status of the recipient. On the other hand, people with *mien-tsu* are expected to receive or present gifts that match their prestigious status. People who wrongly behave in gift giving will end up having to break their relationships with the recipients.

The Concept of Guanxi. The word *guanxi* has literally the same meaning of "relationship" in English. In reality, it has a much more sophisticated meaning than "relationship." It consists of two Chinese characters, *guan* and *xi* that mean "relating" and "bonding" respectively. Hence, *guanxi* virtually means the social relationship between two persons under a particular bonding. Originally, this bonding referred to one of Confucius' five cardinal bonds (*wu lun*) which included the bonds between sovereign and minister, father and son, husband and wife, old and young, and friend and friend (Hchu and Yang 1972). However, these bonds have been further extended to include the following:

- Relatives in the same kinship system–these include uncles, aunts, cousins, nephews and nieces, etc.
- Townsmen–those who live in or come from the same town.
- Classmates–those who study together, but those in the same class or cohort have closer bonding.
- Colleagues–those who worked or are working in the same firm, or even in the same business unit.
- Heirs of friends for more than two generations.
- People with the same hobbies such as collecting stamps, fishing, writing, etc.
- Past superiors–those who had supervised oneself.
- Past subordinates–those who had worked under oneself.
- Those taught by the same teacher.
- Past students taught by oneself.
- Members of the same school or clan.

- Acquaintances, friends or close friends–those who do not belong to the first eleven types but still remain contacts or close contacts with each other.

These bonds address the similarity between two parties in terms of origin and serve to remove doubt, create trust and form close relationships between parties (Hinde 1987). In the Chinese literature about Chinese cultural values, they are called the twelve commonalties.

These bonds have served effectively to control social behavior in society. The Chinese must observe and act according to the norm prescribed for each bond. Various bonds indicate different levels of *guanxi*. Normally, the level of *guanxi* between father and son is closer than that between friends. When asked about his response if he would bear witness when his father had stolen a sheep, Confucius explained, "the father conceals the misconduct of the son, and the son conceals the misconduct of the father" (Confucian Analects, XIII, Ch. 18). Confucius refused to whistle-blow because of the close relationship between father and son. A son is not in the position to bear witness. As such, it is understood that a gift presented to someone with a close relationship tends to be different from that presented to someone with a distant relationship. For example, Kipnis (1997) in his study of Chinese gift giving observed that gift giving for celebrating the birth of a relative is two or three times more expensive than friends.

The Concept of Reciprocity (bao). Before we proceed to examine the Chinese concept of reciprocity, it seems necessary to define the concept in general terms. Reciprocity can be summarized by three interrelated aspects of social action between two individuals (Lebra 1976), bilateral contingency, interdependence for mutual benefit and equality of exchanged values. Firstly when a person does a favor for another person, he/she may oblige the recipient to repay. This is bilateral contingency. However, there is a difference between Chinese and Western cultures regarding the time when a favor should be repaid. Chinese believe that repayment should not be made immediately, but at the right time when both givers and recipients will be benefited. Westerners tend to repay more quickly to relieve their tension.

Second, the rationale for a person giving something to another person may be the intention to obtain something else that is needed from the recipient. Chinese givers often do not have an explicit and specific purpose at the time when gifts are presented. However, they may have a vague idea of establishing a good relationship with the recipient in the long term.

Third, the reciprocal process will eventually approach a converged value. In other words, what a person gives will be the equivalent to what he/she receives from the same recipient in the long run. These symmetric aspects of reciprocity, mostly emphasized by Western scholars, have been regarded as "sociological dualism" and "mutual legal obligations of repaying" (Malinowski 1959). In particular, Gouldner (1960) insisted on the equality of exchanged values in the pursuit of fair distribution of rights and duties.

In the Chinese cultural setting, reciprocity immediately suggests the concepts of *un* and *qui* as two complementary concepts of reciprocity (*bao*). *Un* literally means "gratitude" and *qui* as "hatred." *Un* is produced when someone does us a favor; *qui* is created when there are grievances. Therefore, the creation of *un* and *qui* must be followed by the emotion of *bao*. This is indicated by the following Chinese proverbial sayings according to Confucius:

1. "if you have received, and never returned, a favor, you are not conforming properly to *Li* (propriety)."
2. "if there is gratitude, repay; if there are animosities, take vengeance."
3. "we are not a gentleman if we don't take revenge; we are not a man if we don't return favor."
4. "receive a peach and return a plum."

These sayings also indicate that *bao* can be either positive or negative. Obviously, the presence of *un* will lead to the positive *bao* while the presence of *qui* will result in negative *bao*. Further, Chinese do not emphasize the symmetry of reciprocity. The value of a gift involved in reciprocal exchanges of favor never remains constant and will continue to grow. The following Chinese proverb indicates that the value of a favor returned is several times as much as the value received. "If you honor me a linear foot, I should in return honor you ten feet."

Recipients face severe peer pressure when they return favors. Unless they repay a favor with greater value than what they have received, they will not be regarded as "gentlemen" and thus will not reach a state of psychological balance. An *un* relationship, once generated by giving and receiving a benefit, will not necessarily compel the receiver-debtor to repay *un* in order to restore balance. The common Chinese saying of "return good with evil" reflects this ungrateful situation.

The concept of reciprocity has particular implications on the practice of gift giving. First, gift giving is a way to establish and maintain a relationship with the gift recipients. Second, reciprocity differs from contractual relationships, in which the rights and obligations of two parties are specified in a legal document (Lebra 1976). Reciprocity is more informal and personal and its effectiveness is very much derived from other parties' memories. Gift giving then serves as an activity to awaken these memories. The more frequent is the activity, the closer is the relationship. Third, Chinese gift givers, different from their Western counterparts, are not looking for immediate repayment of gratitude. Rather, they would enjoy maintaining such an imbalance that brings to them pride and luck. Hence, the Chinese say, "it is always more fortunate to be a gift giver than a recipient." However, the psychology of gift recipients tends to be different, yet still dissimilar to that of the Westerners. Gift recipients are usually eager to repay. Chinese tend to repay with a greater favor than they received. They do not intend to repay immediately as the Western counterparts who try to extricate themselves from the emotional entanglement. Instead, they prefer to wait for a better time to come. Hence, a good occasion will serve to magnify the value of a gift to a recipient.

PERCEIVED IMPORTANCE OF OCCASIONS

Evidence has shown that situations may exert influence directly on behavior (Sheth 1972, Triandis, Bearden and Woodside 1976a, 1978b). A situation may put restrictions upon a consumer who would emotionally respond according to his interpretation of the situation (Lutz and Kakkar 1974, Belk 1975). Using the same analogy, an occasion that can be considered as a situation may have significant impact on behavior such as gift giving. Belk (1973) examined the frequency of all gift giving and concluded that Birthday and Christmas are the two most important occasions for gift giving, followed by Mother's Day/Father's Day, Wedding Anniversary, Graduation, and others. Bussey (1967) reported similar findings for birthdays and Christmas in Britain except in the reverse order of prevalence. The reverse order of prevalence indicates a difference in the perceived importance of occasions for a gift-giving activity and may be attributable to cultural differences. In fact, occasions for gift giving may vary across cultures. Obviously, Chinese New Year is an important occasion for gift giving in the the Chinese culture, but would not be one in the West.

SYMBOLISM OF GIFTS

There is meaning present in the consumption patterns of others (Belk, Bahn and Mayer 1982). Consumption symbolism is to make inferences about others based on their choices of consumption objects. In particular, symbols are potentially powerful communication devices in gift giving, but many symbols are culture-specific (Cohen 1996). Givers tend to look for gifts for two reasons. On the one hand, the gifts may reflect or symbolize their self-image or intention of giving gifts, for example, to show the recipients that they are generous. On the other hand, the gifts are indicative of the social status of recipients. When the recipient considers himself to be a renowned businessperson, an expensive gift may serve to match the recipient's status.

Thus, gifts do not necessarily symbolize the self-image or intention of the givers but those of the recipients instead.

GIFT-GIVING INVOLVEMENT

Belk (1988) considered gift selection as a more involving activity than making a comparable selection for personal use. He classified involvement in gift giving into two types. One is item specific and the other is purchase situation-specific. Item-specific involvement has been labeled differently in the literature. Howard and Sheth (1969) named it as "importance of purchase," Lastovika (1976) as "issue involvement," Rothchild (1977) as "enduring involvement" and Clarke and Belk (1979) as "product involvement." All these indicate that consumers are more concerned about the item and interested in the purchase outcome (Belk 1988). The second type deals with task involvement that arises from a consumer's goal in a particular shopping or usage situation. For example, the goal may be "finding a sweater which is the least expensive in town."

These two types of involvement tend to co-vary with each other. For example, if the gift giver has an important goal of getting an impressive ornament for his wife's birthday, he will attempt to select a gift item that is high in involvement. This indicates the effect of gift-giving involvement on gift purchasing.

AROUSAL TO GIFT GIVING

In consumer behavior, arousal is always regarded as an important variable in information processing and persuasion (Assael 1992, Sanbonmatsu and Kardes 1987). Engel et al. (1993) defined it as a person's degree of alertness to information in the persuasion process. In other words, the level of arousal may be subject to message elements other than the product claims in situations in which consumers receive persuasive communications. Using the same analogy, givers in gift giving may be aroused to purchase by gift-giving situations and the symbolism of gifts. In addition, the level of *guanxi* between the givers and recipients may serve as a moderating variable affecting the level of arousal to gift giving. That is, given a particular situation such as a birthday, the level of arousal may be further augmented if it is the birthday of the giver's father.

GIFT PURCHASING

Gift purchasing refers to the purchase behavior of the givers. When a giver has determined to purchase a gift for a particular person, the following two decisions must be made:

- What are the brands/products that the giver prefers to purchase?
- Where does the giver purchase the gift?

The literature on brand choice reveals that there is a strong influence of family members on brand choice of cars (Day 1970). Monroe and Guiltiman (1975) reckoned that consumers select a store first and then determine the product to be purchased within the store. In addition, they also considered that store choice is affected by the attitude towards store which, in turn, is influenced by the store's image. However, recent studies have seldom considered brand/store choice for a product that the purchaser buys for someone to consume or use. In a gift-purchasing situation, at least two parties, the givers and the recipients, are to be considered in many purchasing situations.

When making these decisions, the givers take into consideration whether the choice of brands/products and the purchase locations are consistent with the gift symbols to be associated and in parallel with the level of *guanxi* with the recipients.

FOCUS GROUP INTERVIEWS AND FINDINGS

An exploratory study was conducted using focus group interviews as the major data collection instrument. Twelve focus group interviews were conducted during 1997. Participants were drawn from all walks of life in Hong Kong but mainly in the age range of twenty to fifty-five. Except for two control groups made up of members from the same genders, all groups were well mixed.

There were eight participants in each focus group. They were recruited and selected through a process of "snowball type of sampling method" to ensure relative homogeneity. Individuals were screened based on their differences in perceptions, experiences, and verbal skills before being selected as participants at various focus group sessions. They were invited to the venue which was conveniently located in the city and all interviews were conducted after office hours. All interviews, except one which served as a demo, were moderated by the same moderator who had taken into account all the key qualifications for conducting focus groups as suggested by Churchill (1979). All the discussions were tape-recorded for later analysis. Each interview ran for about two hours.

Findings of focus group discussions in this study indicated that gift-giving occasions among the Hong Kong Chinese could be classified into four categories: achievement, special, recurring, and others. Achievement-related occasions refer to those events where the recipients have accomplished something in their career, leading to an honorable award. For example, we have been invited to a banquet to celebrate someone who has just received The Order of Grand Bauhinia from the Chief Executive of the Hong Kong Special Administrative Region; or your friends has just received the title of chartered accountant. Special occasions are unique events but have nothing to do with achievement. For example, a Chinese 60th year birthday is an extremely special and important event. According to the Chinese calendar, the name of a year repeats every sixty years. Thus, Chinese people believe that one is entering another cycle of life in the 60th year. Celebration is needed for at least two reasons. First, sixty years of age is regarded as old age, which is the time to enjoy the fortune one has accumulated. Second, Chinese people believe that starting a new cycle at the age of sixty makes one as weak and vulnerable as a baby. Having a banquet and receiving gifts and good words from friends and relatives serve as a booster to ensure longevity.

Recurring occasions refers to those situations which occur repeatedly at constant intervals. Examples of this category are Chinese New Year, birthdays, Christmas parties and wedding anniversaries, which may be celebrated every year. Other occasions refer to those not falling into any of these three categories. In particular, occasions in this "other" category are more causal and spontaneous in nature. For example, the giver purchases a gift because he came across something that the recipient, his good friend, may like or need.

As for the symbols of gifts, findings of the focus group interviews could be summarized into two categories:

- Givers: Meaningfulness, Good intention, and Generosity; and
- Recipients: Prestige, Success, and Expensiveness.

From the givers' viewpoint, gifts serve various purposes. One of them is to associate with the good meanings for the particular occasions for which gifts are presented. For example, giving a turtle for a birthday of a mature person has a denotative meaning of long life. Gifts are also indicative of the good purpose that the givers would like to achieve. Sometimes, givers want to show that they care about the recipients by presenting gifts that are appropriate for those occasions. In the Chinese society, givers always want to show that they possess some particular virtue. Generosity tends to be a popular and common one.

A gift presented should be indicative of the giver understanding of the recipient personality traits or social status. Thus when the recipient receives the gift, he will be happy with the gift itself as well as its symbolic meanings.

From the recipients' perspective, we have found three important symbols in gift giving in Chinese societies: prestige, success, and expensiveness. Recipients are looking for gifts with some prestige attached to them, perhaps because of the high quality or high social value of the gifts. Success is associated with gifts which symbolize some kind of achievement that recipients have been trying to attain. Gifts which cost a lot of money would fit the symbolism of expensiveness.

A MODEL OF GIFT PURCHASING

Sherry, McGrath and Levy (1993) typologized gift giving into three basic components, gifts, givers and recipients, and situational conditions. The above discussion indicates that these three components cannot serve to explain adequately gift-purchasing behavior in Chinese communities. In this section, we present a more comprehensive model that encompasses the following six components:

1. Chinese cultural values.
2. Perceived importance of occasion.
3. Symbolism of the gift.
4. Involvement with recipients.
5. Arousal to gift giving.
6. Gift purchasing.

The model of Chinese cultural values and gift giving is depicted in Figure 1.

The first component is an independent variable while the last five components are dependent variables. Symbolism of the gift and arousal to gift giving are two major dependent variables. Symbolism of the gift is related directly to and is a mediating variable of gift purchasing. In this model, arrows that show the direction of postulated influence indicate causality between components. The model assumes that there is a one-way flow of causation. The solid lines together with the arrows hierarchically show how determinants cause or influence other determinants. As this paper reports on only the initial phase of a comprehensive study to explore Chinese cultural values and consumer behavior, the model does not address attitudinal or behavioural variables that will have an impact on Chinese cultural values. Hence, there is no feedback flow in the model. The model of propositions, as indicated by the links between the constructs, reflect a number of the potential relationships that are supported by the literature. Many of these relationships were generated from the focus group interviews which provided additional information and antecedents of the relationship between gift purchasing and certain Chinese rules.

FIGURE 1. A Model of Chinese Cultural Values and Gift Giving

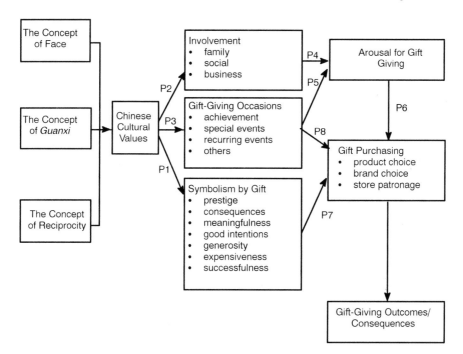

Based on the literature review and focus group interviews, eight proposi- tions are developed in three different categories as follows:

I. Chinese Cultural Values as Social Referents

P1: The greater the importance placed on Chinese cultural values (in terms of face, reciprocity and *guanxi*), the more concerned the giver is about the symbolism of the gift.

Higher enthusiasm about Chinese cultural values increases the givers' consideration of the symbolism of the gift. Choosing the right gift which carries appropriate symbolism is linked to the outcome or con- sequences of the gift-giving and receiving behaviors. This is an area deserving special attention. A great deal of studies examined product choices and the criteria involved (Bettman 1989; Brucks 1985; Park et al. 1994). Many cross-cultural researchers agreed that it is essential to indigenize consumer behavior model to take into consideration the diversity of the cultural impact. The applicability of such on gift giving is therefore proposed.

P2: The greater the importance placed on Chinese cultural values (in terms of face, reciprocity and *guanxi*), the higher the level of involvement in gift purchasing.

Chinese cultural values influence the level of involvement of the givers in gift purchasing for the recipients. The more an individual respects and recognizes Chinese cultural values, the more they are likely to be attentive towards the intrinsic involvement of gift purchasing. Intrinsic involvement is basically the perceived link between the purchase and one's self-concept (Johnson and Eagley 1990; Richins and Bloch 1986). It is the intrinsic importance to the giver of gift, which often ties in with the family, social, or business relations with the receiver.

P3: The greater the importance placed on Chinese cultural values (in terms of face, reciprocity and *guanxi*), the more concerned the giver is about the importance of gift-giving occasions.

Chinese cultural values may affect the perceived importance of gift-giving occasions. The importance placed upon Chinese cultural values enhances the gift-giving situation because of the belief that the effort will bring favorable outcomes in terms of face, reciprocity and *guanxi*. This is in line with the concept of situational involvement, dealing with the linkage between the gift-giving situation and the outcomes or consequences of the situation (Schmidt and Spreng 1996).

II. Arousal to Gift Giving

P4: Higher level of involvement in gift giving increases the arousal to gift giving.

The notion of consumer involvement was first introduced by Krugman (1965) and involvement is viewed as the perceived personal relevance of the situation (Celsi and Olson, 1988), in this case, gift giving. Consumer behavior theories suggest that consumers are more aroused when involvement is high (Engel et al. 1993; Hawkins et al. 1986). Therefore, the higher the level of involvement in gift giving, the higher the level of arousal.

P5: Greater perceived importance of the occasion increases the arousal to gift giving.

Greater perceived importance of the occasion enhances greater attention and information processing leading to increases in one's motivation to give a gift. That is, the more important the occasion is, the higher the level of arousal to gift giving.

III. Gift Purchasing

P6: The higher the level of arousal, the greater the desire for achieving the optimal gift-purchasing decision.

The level of arousal has a positive effect on the gift-purchasing decision. The higher the level of arousal, the stronger would be the desire for an optimal gift-giving decision rather than just an acceptable one. Swan (1969) found that making the optimal decision required significantly more complex considerations. This would imply that the gift-purchasing decision would consider more products and brands in the evoked set, more prestigious brands to be purchased, and a greater number of types of retail outlets to be considered for patronage.

P7: The greater the emphasis placed on the symbolism of the gift, the greater the desire for achieving the optimal gift-purchasing decision.

Consideration of the symbolism of the gift may influence the gift-purchasing decision. That is, the more concerned the giver is about the symbolism of gift, the more products in the choice set, the more prestigious is the brand to be purchased and the retail outlet to be patronized.

P8: The more important a gift-giving occasion is, the greater the desire for achieving the optimal gift-purchasing decision.

Consideration of a gift-giving occasion may influence the gift-purchasing decision. That is, the more important a gift-giving occasion is perceived by the giver, the more prestigious is the brand to be purchased or the retail outlet to be patronized.

CONCLUSION

A model of gift-purchasing behaviour with Chinese cultural values as a major construct has been developed. In this paper, according to Yau's work, three Chinese cultural values: face, *guanxi* and reciprocity were identified to have an impact on (product) involvement, gift-giving occasions, and the symbolism of a gift. A total of eight propositions were eventually stipulated for empirical testing. It is expected that in order to test the model and its propositions, a full factorial design that takes into consideration the gift-giving occasions, the symbolism of the gift and the level of *guanxi* between givers and recipients is necessary. Other cultural values such as face and reciprocity (Yau 1988), gift purchasing and arousal will then be operationalized accordingly. This paper shows a case of applying Chinese cultural values in explaining gift-purchasing behavior. However, Chinese cultural values can be extended to other areas in marketing as indicated by Yang (1991) and Yau (1994). These applications would be very unique and worth exploring especially in compatible situations across various cultures, despite difficulties in research methodologies.

Earlier cross-cultural research has been full of sweeping generalities that have often been misused to stereotype people and ended up being of little use in explaining or predicting social behavior in various cultures (Yang et al. 1989, Yau 1994b). Two important questions are raised:

1. Are there universal social behaviors or behavioral rules?
2. Are there direct relationships between cultural determinants and specific social behaviors?

In studying cultural influences on social behavior, antecedents and mediating variables are important to ensure solid concepts and theories. Cultural value systems always have their ecological and subsistent background and their historical development. Cross-cultural studies would only be useful if they were based on well-conceived hypotheses that are derived through a good understanding of how cultural determinants are derived and how they influence behavioral dispositions in general. Two major points are worth noting:

1. In cross-cultural studies, some scholars look at the culture of an ethnic group (or national cultural as it appears in many international business texts) as unique (Bond, 1991) while others reckon there are differences within a culture (Buckley and Brooke, 1992). Cross-cultural studies should take the approach of studying both the similarities and differences among cultures on relative and average scales.
2. For marketers, there is a tendency to assume cultural similarity among cultures unless it is proved otherwise as it is more cost and resource efficient to employ a set of global strategies. The concept of segmentation, the impact of multinational firms, and the influence of information technology are all supports to make particular segments in various ethnic groups homogeneous in terms of consumer behavior.

Unless the ambiguous concepts intrinsic to cross-cultural studies and their marketing implications are theoretically refined, adequately operationalised and tested with sound methodologies, the results may not benefit the body of knowledge in the literature.

REFERENCES

Assael, H. (1992), *Consumer Behavior and Marketing Action*, 4th edition, Boston: PWS-Kent Publishing Co.

Baumeister, R. F. and Tice, D. M. (1986), "Four Selves, two motives, and a substitute process self-regulation model," in R. F. Baumeister (Ed.), *Public self and private self.* New York: Springer-Verlag.

Bearden, W. D. and Woodside, A. G. (1976a), "Commentaries on Belk, 'Situation Variables and Consumer Behavior.'" *Journal of Consumer Research*, 2, December, p. 165.

Bearden, W. D. and Woodside, A. G. (1976b), "Interaction of Consumption Situations and Brand Attitudes," *Journal of Applied Psychology*, 61, 6, pp. 764-769.

Belk, W. R. (1975), "Situation Variables and Consumer Behavior," *Journal of Consumer Research*, 2, December, pp. 157-167.

Belk, R. W. (1988), "Possessions and the Extended Self," *Journal of Consumer Research*, 15, September, pp. 139-168.

Belk, R. W., Bahn, K. D., and Mayer, R. N. (1982), "Developmental Recognition of Consumption Symbolism," *Journal of Consumer Research*, 9, June, pp. 4-17.

Bettman, J. (1979), *An Information Processing Theory of Consumer Choice*, Reading, MA: Addison-Wesley.

Bond, Michael H. and Hofstede, G. (1989), "The Cash Value of Confucian Values," *Human Systems Management*, 8 (3): pp. 195-199.

Buckley, Peter J. and Brooke, Michael Z. (1992), *International Business Studies: An Overview*, Blackwell, p. 273.

Bussey, J. et al. (1967), "Patterns of Gift-Giving," Management Centre, University of Bradford.

Brucks, M. (1985), "The Effect of Product Class Knowledge on Information Search Behavior," *Journal of Consumer Research*, 12, June, pp. 1-15.

Campbell, Donald T. and Fiske, Donald W. (1959), "Convergent and Discriminant Validation by the Multitrait-Multimethod Matrix," *Psychological Bulletin*, 56, pp. 81-105.

Celsi, R. and Olson, J. (1988), "The Role of Involvement in Attention and Comprehension Processes," *Journal of Consumer Research*, 15, September, pp. 210-224.

Chow, M. L. and Ho, D. Y. F. (1992), "The Content and Social Operation of Face: A cross-cultural point of view," in Yang, K. S. and Yu, O. B. (Eds.), *Chinese Psychology and Behavior*, (in Chinese), pp. 205-254.

Churchill, Gilbert A., Jr. (1979), *Marketing Research: Methodological Foundations*. The Dryden Press.

Clarke, K., and Belk, R. W. (1979), "The Effects of Product Involvement and Task Definition on Anticipated Consumer Effort," in *Advances in Consumer Research*, pp. 313-318.

Cohen, J. (1996), "The Search for Universal Symbols: The Case of Right and Left," *Journal of International Consumer Marketing*, 8, (3, 4), pp. 187-210.

Confucius: The Analects, Book XIII, Chapter 18, (1992) translated by D. C. Lau, 2nd edition, The Chinese University Press, Hong Kong.

Day, George S. (1970), *Buyer Attitudes and Brand Choice*, New York: Free Press.

Engel, J. F., Blackwell, R. D. and Miniard, P. (1993), *Understanding the Consumer*, 7th edition, Fort Worth: The Dryden Press.

Gouldner, A. (1960), "The norm of reciprocity: A preliminary statement," *American Sociological Review*, 25, pp. 1976-1977.

Hawkins, D., Best, R. and Coney, K. (1986), *Consumer Behavior Strategy: Implications for Marketing Strategy*, Plano, TX: Business Publications.

Hchu, H. Y. and Yang, K. S. (1972), "Individual Modernity and Psychogenic Needs," in Li, Y. Y. and Yang, K. S. (Eds.), *Symposium on the Character of the Chinese*, Taipei: Inst. Ethnol. Academic Sincica, pp. 381-410 (in Chinese).

Hinde, Robert A. (1987), *Individuals, Relationships and Culture*, Cambridge University Press, Chapter 2.

Ho, David Y. F. (1976), "On the Concept of Face," *American Journal of Sociology*, 801, pp. 867-884.

Ho, David Y. F. (1979), "Psychological Implications of Collectivism: With Special Reference to the Chinese Case and Maoist Dialectics," in Eckensberger, L. H., Lonner, W. L. and Poortinga, Y. H. (Eds.), *Cross-cultural Contributions to Psychology*, Netherlands: Swets and Zeitlinger, pp. 143-150.

Ho, David Y. F. (1988), "Asian Psychology: A Dialogue on Indigenization and Beyond," in Paranjpe, A. C., Ho, David Y. F. and Rieber, R. W. (Eds.), *Asian Contribution to Psychology*, N.Y.: Praeger.

Hofstede, G. (1980), *Cultural Consequences*, London: Sage Publications.

Hsu, F. L. K. (1970), *Americans and Chinese: Passage to Differences*, 3rd edition, Honolulu: The University of Hawaii.

Hsu, F. L. K. (1971), "Filial Piety in Japan and China: Borrowing, Variation and Significance," *Journal of Comparative Family Studies*, 2, pp. 67-74.

Hu, H. C. (1944), "The Chinese Concept of Face," *American Anthropologist*, 46 (January-March), pp. 45-64.

Inkeles, A. and Levinson, D. L. (1954), "National Character: the Study of Model Personality and Socio-cultural System," in Lindzey, G. (Ed.), *Handbook of Social Psychology*, 4, Reading: Mass: Addison Wesley.

Johnson, B. and Eagley, A. (1990), "Involvement and Persuasion: Types, Traditions, and the Evidence," *Psychological Bulletin*, 107, June, pp. 74-81.

Kindle, T. (1982), "A Partial Theory of Chinese Consumer Behavior: Marketing Strategy Implications," *Hong Kong Journal of Business Management*, 1, pp. 97-109.

Kipnis, A. R. (1997), *Producing Guanxi*, Durham: Duke University Press.

Kluckhohn, F. R. and Strodtdeck, F. L. (1961), *Variations in Value Orientations*, Evanston, IL: Row-Peterson.

Krugman, H. (1965), "The Impact of Television Advertising: Leaning Without Involvement," *Public Opinion Quarterly*, 29, Fall, pp. 249-356.

Lastovika, J. L. (1976), "An Exploratory Multidimensional Scaling Study of Involvement with Products and Services," mimeographed paper (University of Illinois).

Lebra, T. S. (1976), *Japanese Patterns of Behavior*, Honolulu: University of Hawaii Press.

Lutz, R. J. and Kakkar, P. (1974), "The Psychological Situation as a Determinant of Consumer Behavior," in Schlinger, M. J. (Ed.), *Advances in Consumer Research*, 2, Ann Arbor: Association of Consumer Research, pp. 370-378.

Mainowski, B. (1959), *Crime and Custom in Savage Society*, Paterson, N. J.: Littlefield.

Monroe, K. B. and Guiltima, J. B. (1975), "A Path-Analytic Exploration of Retail Patronage Influences," *Journal of Consumer Research*, 2, June, p. 21.

Park, C., Mothersbaugh, D. and Feick, L. (1994), "Consumer Knowledge Assessment," *Journal of Consumer Research*, 21, June, pp. 71-82.

Parsons, T. and Shils, E. A. (1951), "Values, Motivates, and Systems of Action," in Parsons, T. and Shils, E. A. (Eds.), *Towards a General Theory of Action*, New York: Harper & Row, pp. 147-234.

Richins, M. and Block, P. (1986), "After the New Year Wears Off: The Temporal Context of Product Involvement," *Journal of Marketing Research*, 13, September, pp. 280-286.

Rothchild, Michael L. (1977), "Advertising Strategies for High and Low Involvement Situations," *Attitude Research Plays for High Stakes* (Eds.), John C. Maloney and Bernard Silverman, Chicago: American Marketing Association.

Ryan, Adrian (1977), "Consumer Gift Buying Behavior: An Exploratory Analysis," *Contemporary Marketing Thought* (Eds.), Danny Bellinger and Bernard Greenberg, Chicago: American Marketing Association, pp. 99-104.

Sahlins, M. D. (1965), "On the sociology of primitive exchange," *The Relevance of Models for Social Anthropology*, Association of Social Anthropologists of the Commonwealth, Monograph 1, New York: Praeger, pp. 139-238.

Sanbonmatsu, D. M. and Kardes, F. R. (1987), "The Effects of Physiological Arousal in Information Processing and Persuasion," *Journal of Consumer Research*, 15 October, pp. 379-385.

Sherry, J. F. Jr., McGrath, M. A. and Levy, S. J. (1993), "The Dark Side of the Gift," *Journal of Business Research*, 28, pp. 225-244.

Sheth, J. N. (1972), "A Field Study of Attitude Structure and Attitude Behavior Relationship," in Sheth, J. N. (Ed.), *Model of Buyer Behavior*, New York: Harper & Row.

Sudman, Seymour (1983), "Applied Sampling," in Rossi, Peter H., Wright, J. D. and Anderson, A. B. (Eds.), *Handbook of Survey Research*, Orlando, FL: Academic Press, pp. 145-194.

Swan, J. (1969), "Experimental Analysis of Predecision Information Seeking," *Journal of Marketing Research*, 6, March, pp. 192-197.

Tedeschi, J. T. (1986), "Private and public experiences and the self," in Baumeister, R. F. (Ed.), *Public self and private self*, New York: Springer-Verlag.

Triandis, H. C. (1978), "Some universals of social behavior," *Personality and Social Psychology Bulletin*, 4, pp. 1-16.

Wright, Peter L. (1973), "The Cognitive Process Mediating Acceptance of Advertising," *Journal of Marketing Research*, 10, pp. 53-62.

Yang, C. F., Ho, S. C. and Yau, H. M. (1989), *Hong Kong Marketing Management at the Crossroad: A Case Analysis Approach*, The Commercial Press (Hong Kong) Ltd. pp. 317-342.

Yang, C. F. (1991), "A Discussion of the Chinese 'self': Theory and Research Direction," in Yang, C. F. and Ko, S. Y. (Eds.), *Chinese: Chinese Mind–Personality and Society*, Taipei: Long Stream Publishing Ltd.

Yang, K. S. (1992), "Chinese Social Orientation: An Aspect of Social Interaction," in Yang, K. S. and You, O. B. (Eds.), *Chinese Psychology and Behavior–Concepts and Methodology*, (in Chinese), Kew Gong Book Ltd., Taiwan, pp. 87-142.

Yau, O. H. M. (1988), "The Chinese Cultural Values: Its Dimensions and Marketing Implications," *European Journal of Marketing*, 22 (5), pp. 44-57.

Yau, O. H. M. (1994a), *Consumer Behavior in China: Customer Satisfaction and Cultural Values*, Routledge, London & New York, pp. 68-93.

Yau, O. H. M. (1994b), "Shaking the World's Academic Orthodoxy: Strategies for a Chinese Paradigm," Keynote Speech at the First South China International Symposium on "Planning, Developing Markets and Information Technology Support: Managing Business in the 1990's," Macau, 28-30 March, 1994.

Index